AF400878

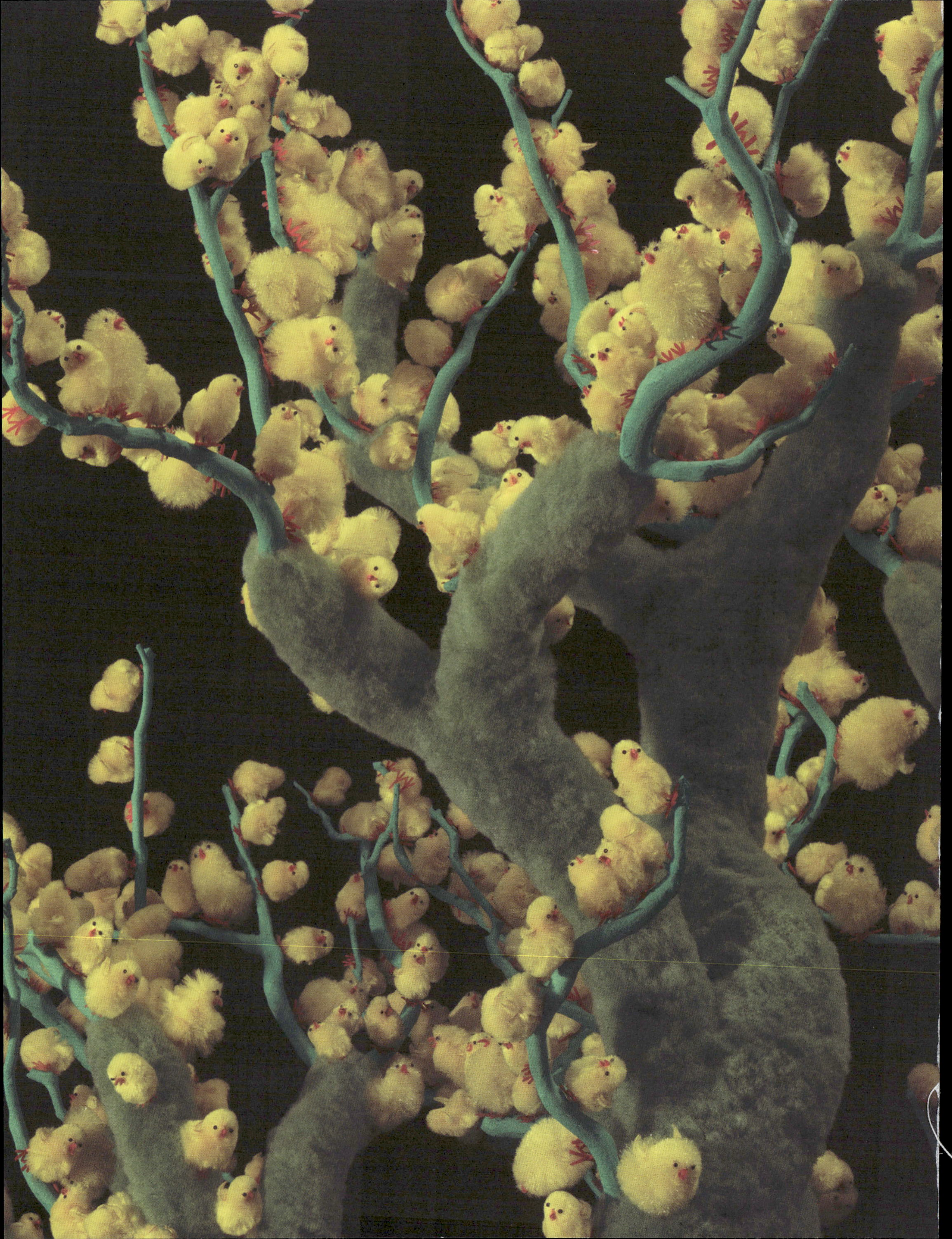

SANDY SKOGLUND
ENCHANTING NATURE

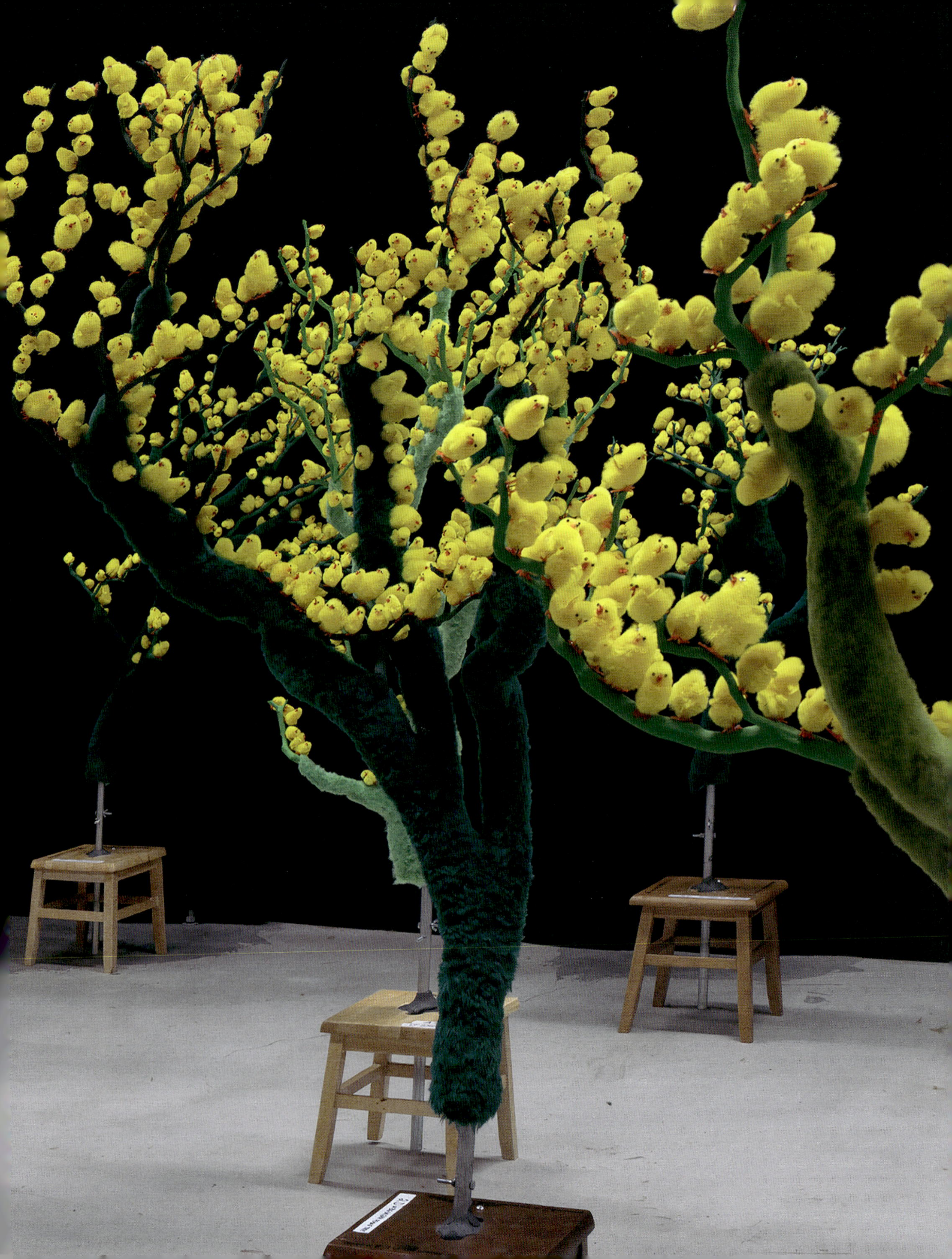

Introduction

The McNay Art Museum's commitment to Sandy Skoglund and her enchanting body of artworks can be traced back over two decades. In 2006, through the efforts of the McNay Contemporary Collectors Forum, the Museum acquired the photograph *Gathering Paradise*, depicting a pink suburban patio overrun with purplish-black squirrels. Three years later, *The Cocktail Party* installation and photograph were gifted to the museum anonymously. A favorite of McNay visitors, the installation includes life-size party guests completely covered in bright orange Cheez Doodles. Most recently, the photograph *Winter* entered the collection as a partial gift of the artist. A frigid blue scene dominates, with a frozen female figure, three menacing owls, and oversize snowflakes completing the tableau.

In addition to these significant acquisitions, Skoglund's works have appeared in numerous collection hangings, while *Winter*—both the installation and photograph—were featured in the McNay's 2021 exhibition *Limitless! Five Women Reshape Contemporary Art*.

It is only fitting that the McNay present a new exhibition of Skoglund's work in 2025. A collaboration between the artist and the museum, *Sandy Skoglund: Enchanting Nature*, brings together two important installations—*Radioactive Cats* (1980) and *Revenge of the Goldfish* (1981)—with a never-before-exhibited installation of *Fresh Hybrid* (2008). In addition to these sculptural works, here Skoglund pushes her approach to exhibiting photographs by creating for the first time monumental wallpaper enlargements of her own artworks. Wallpaper allows viewers to see details usually indiscernible in the framed photographs, revealing how Skoglund manipulates materials to accomplish a wide range of visual effects. In *Enchanting Nature*, photographic imagery and gallery architecture merge to offer an entirely new way of experiencing Sandy Skoglund's art.

This volume, bearing the same title as the McNay's exhibition, serves not only as the exhibition catalogue, but also includes exhibition installation views of wallpaper enlargements from Skoglund's iconic photographs. The wallpaper's ephemerality, existing only for the duration of the exhibition, makes this documentation even more important. Other artworks appearing in *Enchanting Nature*—like *The Outtakes* series—also appear in these pages.

Included in this publication is a conversation between editor and writer Laura van Straaten and the artist. Skoglund's candid responses to van Straaten's questions about what inspires and motivates the artwork, along with Skoglund's descriptions of her studio practice, give the reader further insight into the artist's working process.

Finally, the entirety of this project would not have been possible without the unparalleled vision and collaborative spirit of Sandy Skoglund herself. The longtime partnership between the artist and the McNay Art Museum is both deepened and expanded through *Sandy Skoglund: Enchanting Nature*.

René Paul Barilleaux
Curator, *Sandy Skoglund: Enchanting Nature*
McNay Art Museum

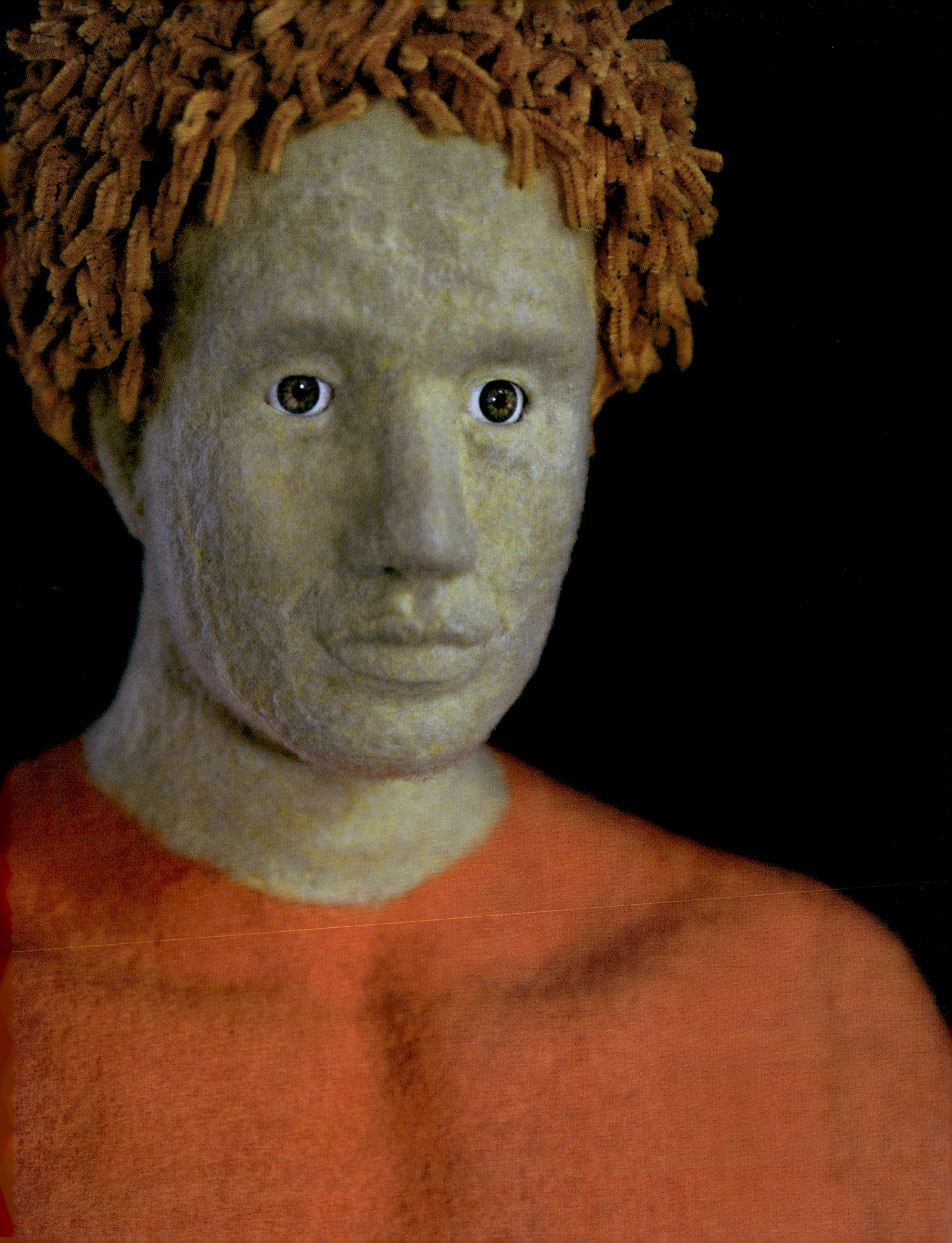

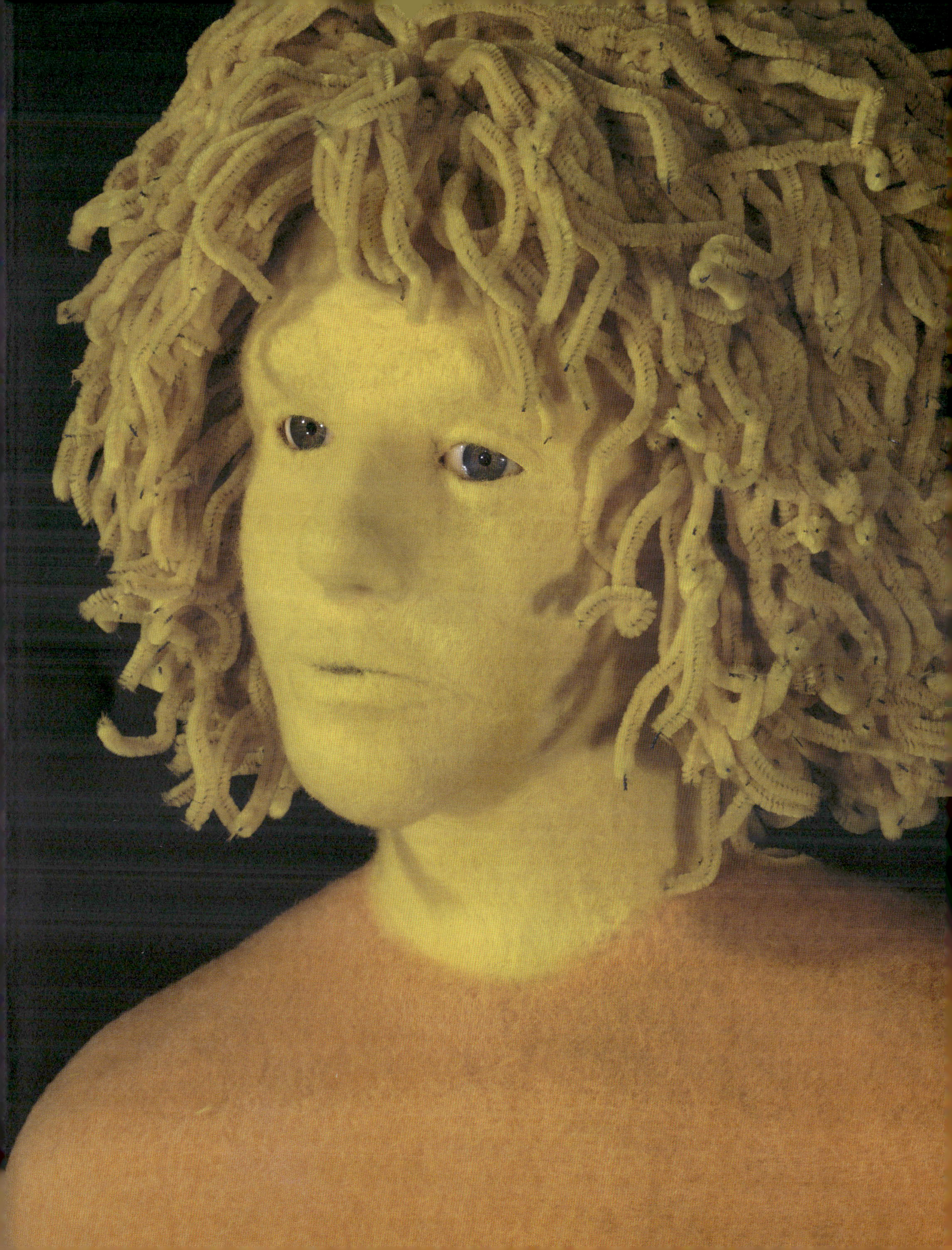

A Conversation

Sandy Skoglund in conversation with journalist Laura van Straaten, a feature writer and contributing editor who has written for many of art publications and sites in the United States and abroad. Van Straaten is a frequent contributor to *The New York Times*, *W Magazine*, and *Town & Country*.

Laura van Straaten (LvS): *How did you come up with the title* Enchanting Nature *for your exhibition at the McNay? What themes were you trying to bring into focus?*

Sandy Skoglund (SS): One of the other titles we considered was *Natural Havoc*. The underlying idea was how nature wreaks havoc when it transforms itself in the quest for survival and its own perpetuation.

With *Enchanting Nature*, we were looking at how "natural" becomes "unnatural" before our eyes, and this does not necessarily portend disaster.

The narrative story of all three installations is the same: the incredible resiliency of nature and how nature's desire to survive is so immense that it changes and evolves into "unnatural" life-forms to perpetuate itself.

In *Radioactive Cats*, the cats are surviving after a nuclear holocaust, and they have turned green and are now radioactive in a radioactive world. Like the dogs of Chernobyl, the cats are normal in a world that has become strange and different. The goldfish in *Revenge of the Goldfish* were cast off as tiny insignificant pets living in a bowl and they grew and evolved in the sewers to take revenge on their keepers. The trees in *Fresh Hybrid* have merged with animals to be able to survive as new life-forms. The cats, the fish, the trees— are all survivors.

LvS: *What do you love about working in installation?*

SS: It doesn't reflect or reveal meaning so much as it stages a place for meaning to unfold, or, even better, allows visitors to construct their own meanings. It's about materials, labor, and the presence of the hand in the making of the work. I see the installation as an open door. The viewer gets

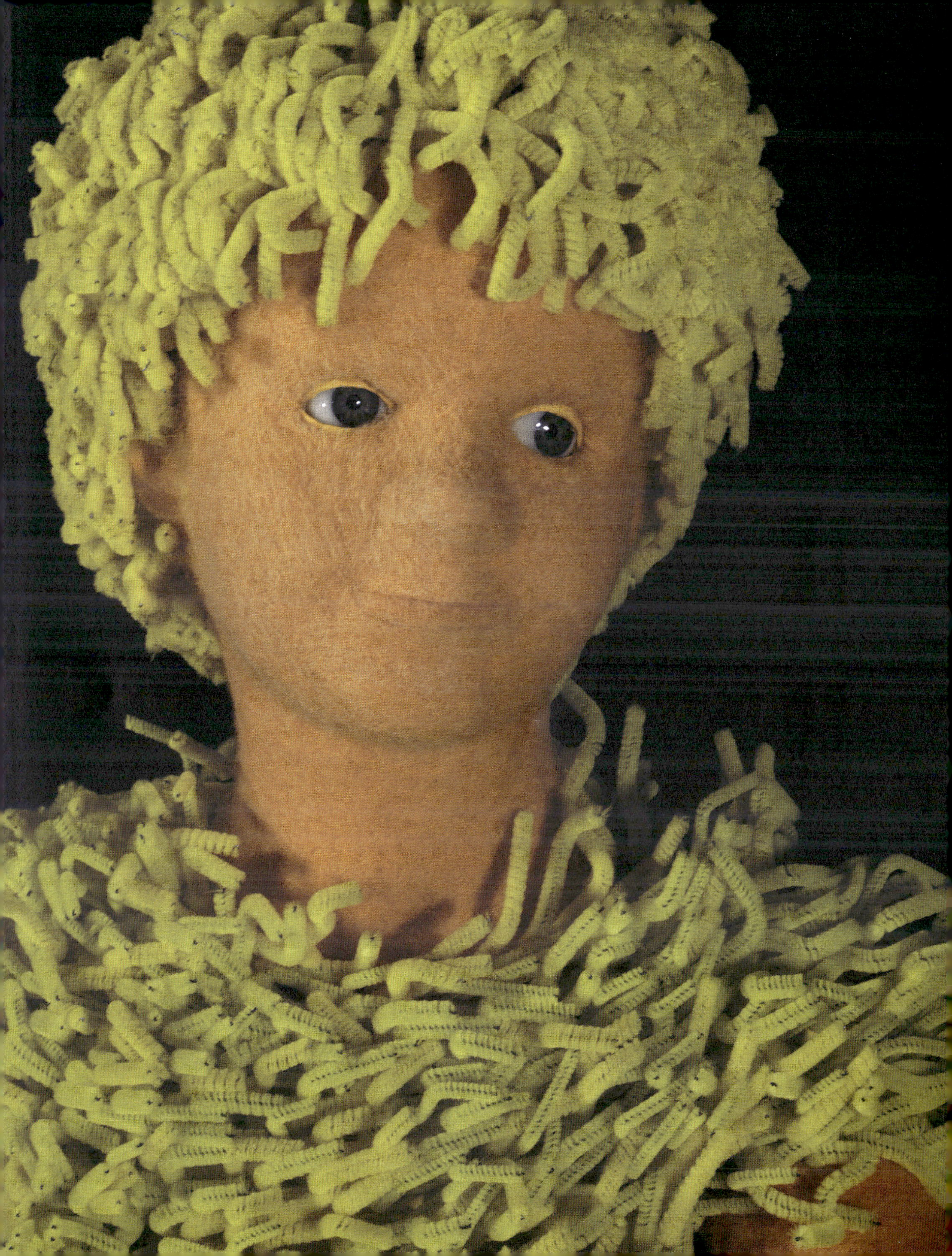

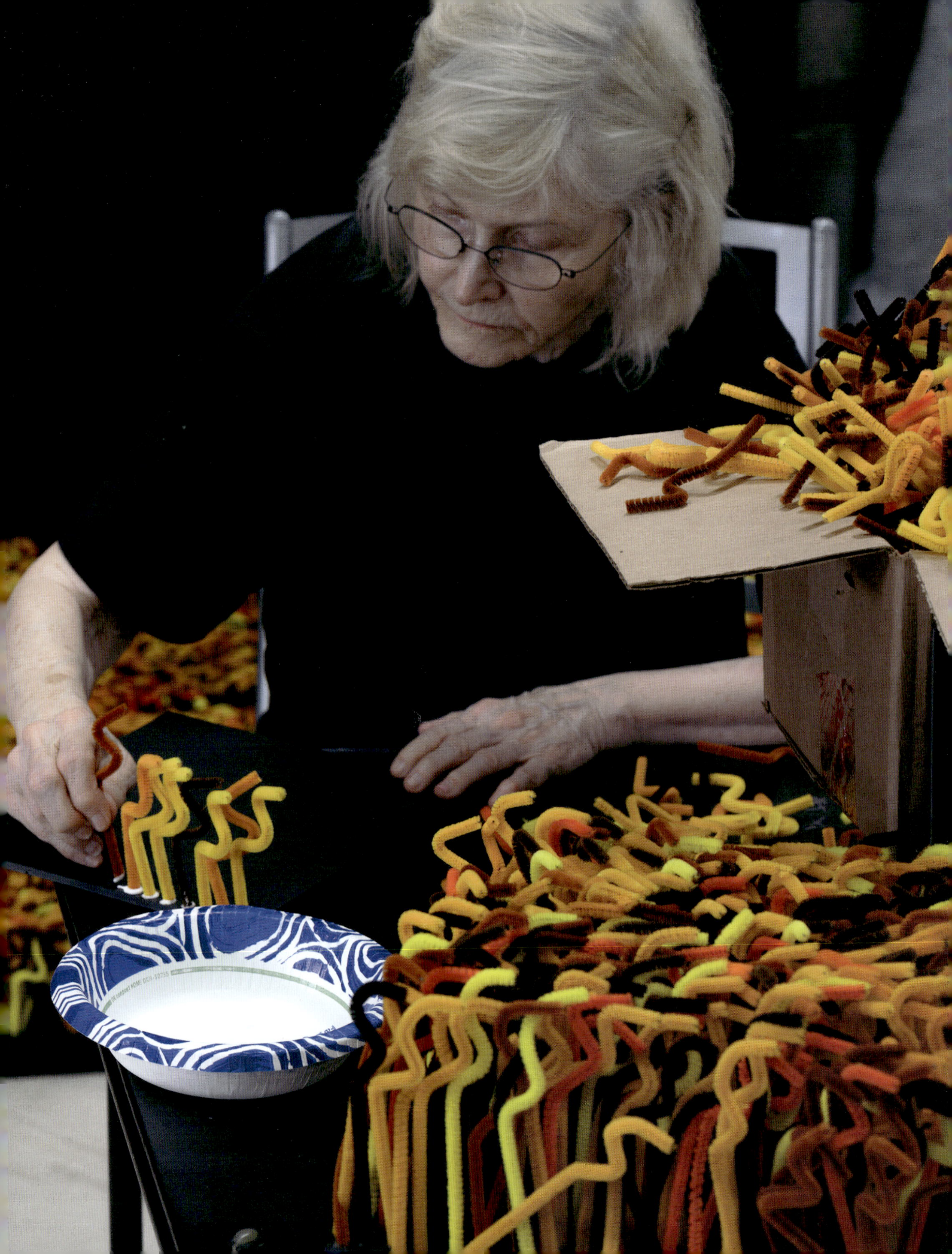

to be among and within the art and to feel like they belong in it.

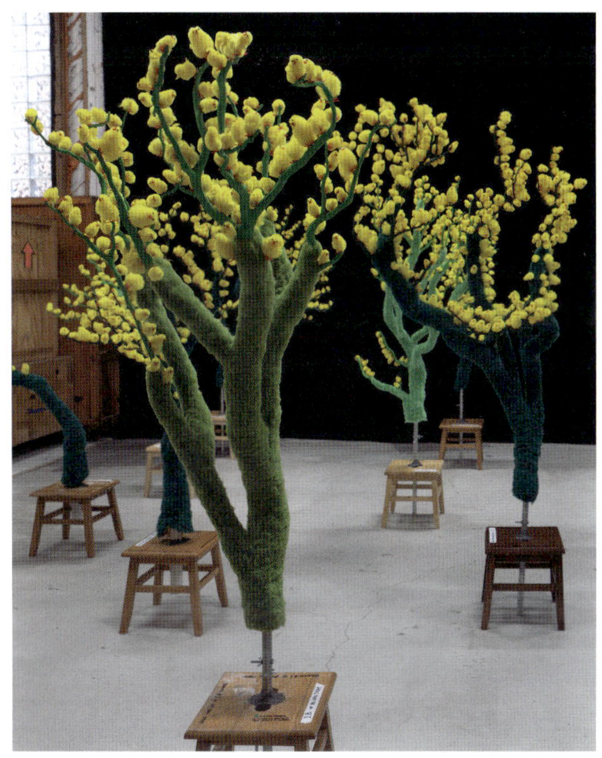

LvS: *In the 70s, you and your husband rented a mobile home on a farm outside of Utica, New York, where you first started experimenting with installation and carefully staged "moments." You used your own body in photographs like* Knees in a Tub *(1977). Your work from that period set the stage for the room-sized installations you'd explore soon after starting in 1979. I keep wondering how the confines of a mobile home might have influenced your transition from contained, all-encompassing domestic spaces, to immersive art installations?*

SS: It wasn't the confines of the mobile home but the feeling of the Formica and plastic paneling that enveloped me. I used my body (in photographs) to give context to these remarkable things, like the matching pink sink and bathtub. I wanted to depict how uncanny and beautiful the artifice was.

LvS: *Let's delve into the 2008 installation* Fresh Hybrid, *because this is the first time the installation has been exhibited outside of your studio.*

SS: When you first visited my studio, I remember you wanted to reach out and touch the materials. I hope the museum visitor feels the same way. *Fresh Hybrid* is fundamentally based in fiber art: the soft chenille texture of the pipe cleaners and chicks, the combed wool on the tree figures. I hope it feels like a visual blizzard of softness.

In *Fresh Hybrid*, everything is waking up, animated. Still photographs can appear very still. I feel like I have to work hard to disrupt the inertia of the sculptural material and the still photograph. The trees are sculpted aggressively, with branches waving around like the arms of an octopus. They carry a display of kitschy chicks erupting in greetings.

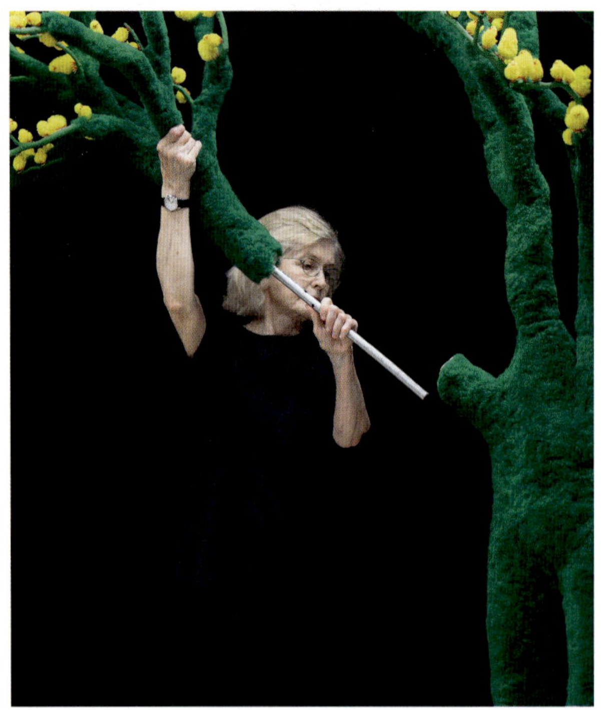

I worked with those chicks because they are not what they seem. They are not without meaning. They are one of the last vestiges of something lost, a spark. Joining the iconography of spark with relentless mass production, the chicks reach out from somewhere we used to be.

I always consider space in my work. The process is a form of time travel. Where am I? Inside or outside? How can I show it? I can only show it by showing what's in it. For me, space must be filled with movement.

LvS: *Walking through your installations, I get this sense of time-lapse—static figures, posed as if caught in action. But there is also an implication of stop-motion animation, the kind where an animator manipulates physical objects in small increments, photographing each scene and combining them sequentially to create the illusion of movement. With that in mind, can you talk about your use of repetition, specifically the creatures and patterns you create?*

SS: I feel like my use of repetition and accumulation is informed by my interest in Conceptual Art in the 70s. There are parallels in music, with Steve Reich, Philip Glass, and others. My conceptual art practice became less nourishing over time, and the repeating elements evolved into more complex forms like cats.

LvS: *Has the warp speed of visual culture changed how you view your own work?*

SS: For me, art is not only about the final image but how you get there. The image is just the tip of the iceberg, the cherry on top of the big pile of stuff I choose to struggle with. I never know where I am going or what the whole image will look like until the very end. The image emerges out of the struggle. That's the thrill of it. After working, working, working, the final image seems to pop up out of nowhere, surprising even me. But how did I get there?

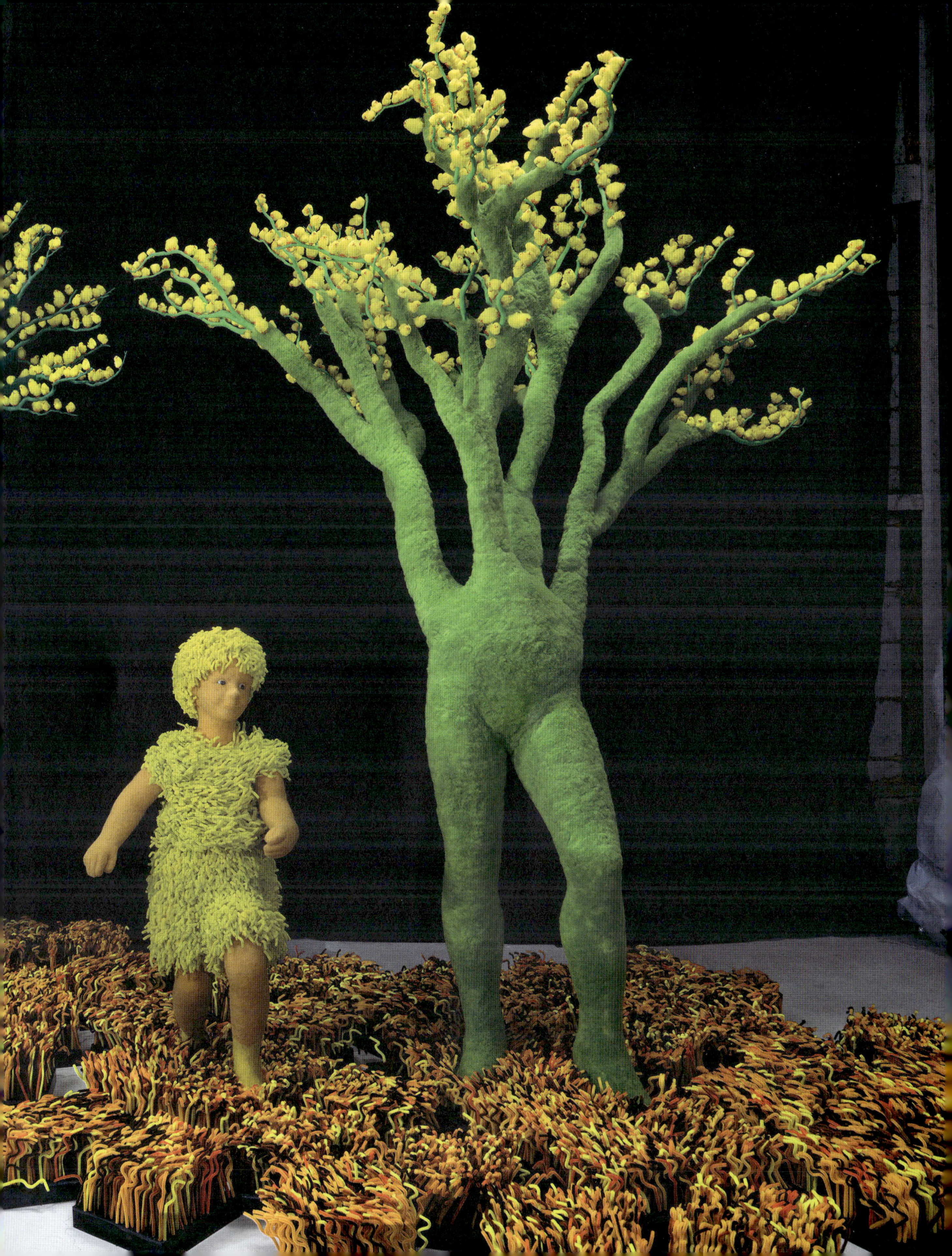

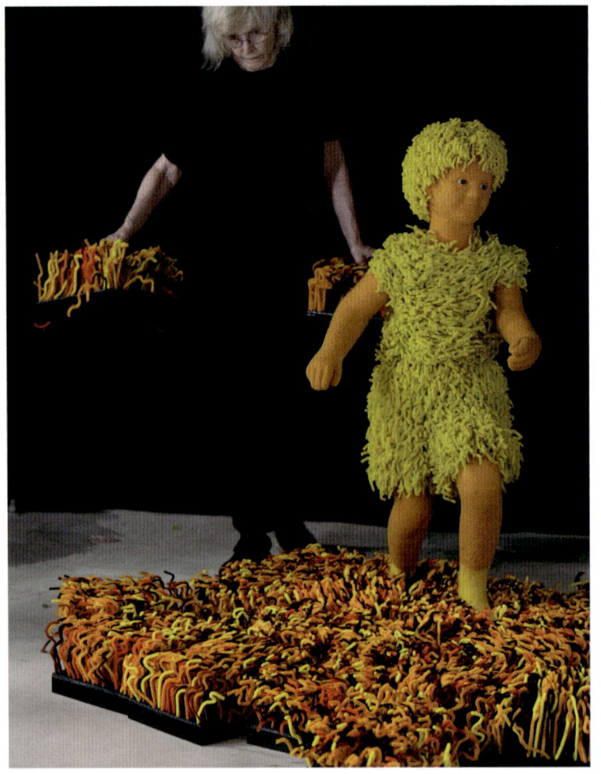

It's always a mystery. Why do we love mysteries? Because they encapsulate and satisfy our eternal struggle to understand. I love struggle. Struggle is dynamic, the opposite of boring. I love working with as many parts of myself as I can. My images are a contradiction. They look imaginary, but they are concrete. Philosophically, my work is just as much about reality as, say, a scientist who conducts test after test in the lab, ending up with a theory they could never have imagined.

LvS: *But the authenticity of the artist's hand, behind the making—*

SS: —is gigantic. I think that is the most important part. In *Fresh Hybrid*, even the way that the pipe cleaners are bent is very me. I physically do as much as I can, but even if someone else, like an assistant in my studio helps, everything is directed by me. And that's why I'm an artist.

LvS: *That makes me think you might have strong feelings about image-making using artificial intelligence (AI)?*

SS: On the facility of image-making and AI, who knows where it is now and where it is headed? I am not against AI, and I might look into using it at some point. But I want to use it in a way that feels unique to me. I also know that I enjoy a struggle, so if the process is quick and easy then it might feel inauthentic.

On the other hand, a quick and easy process might be liberating and so new that it would feel like a new form of authenticity.

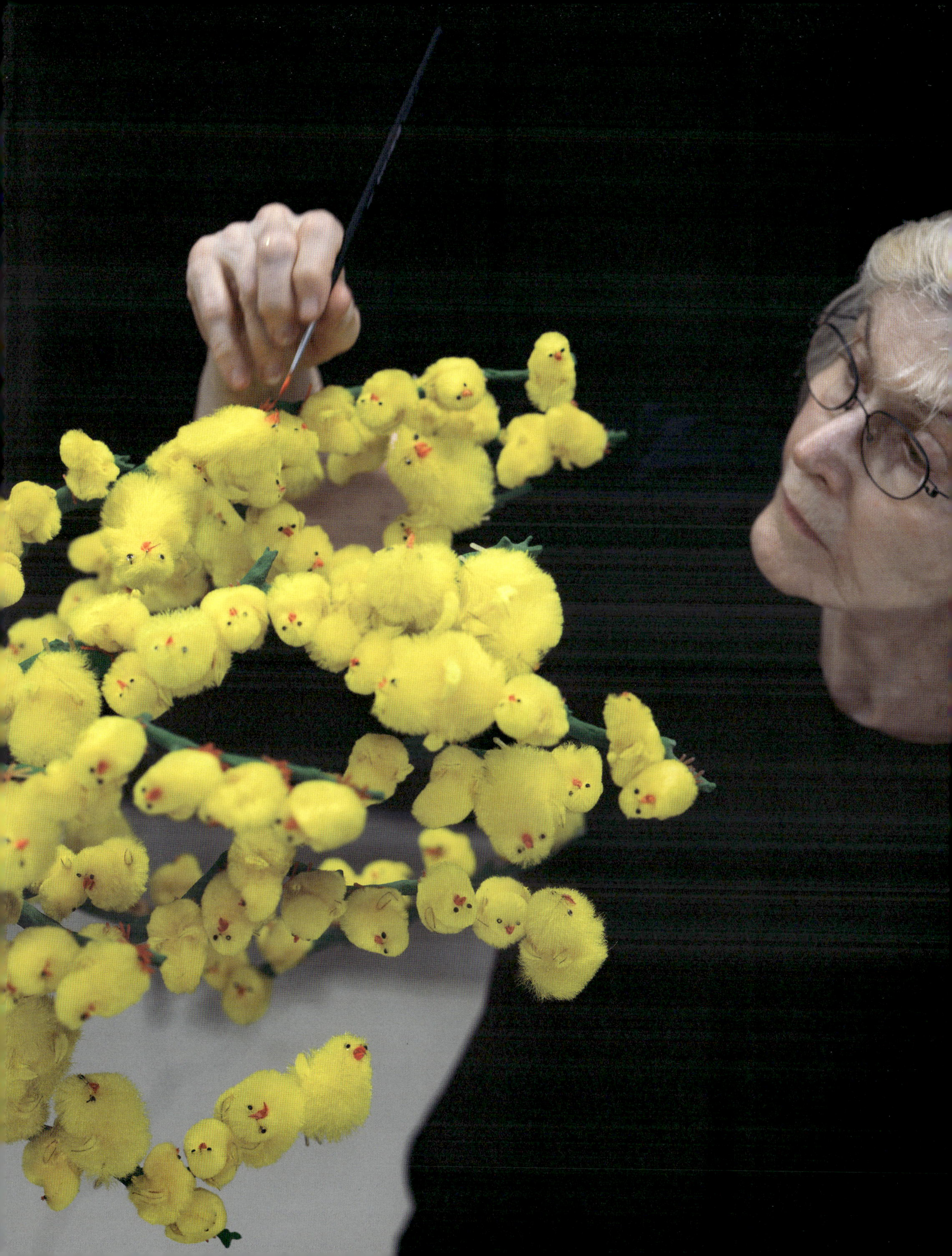

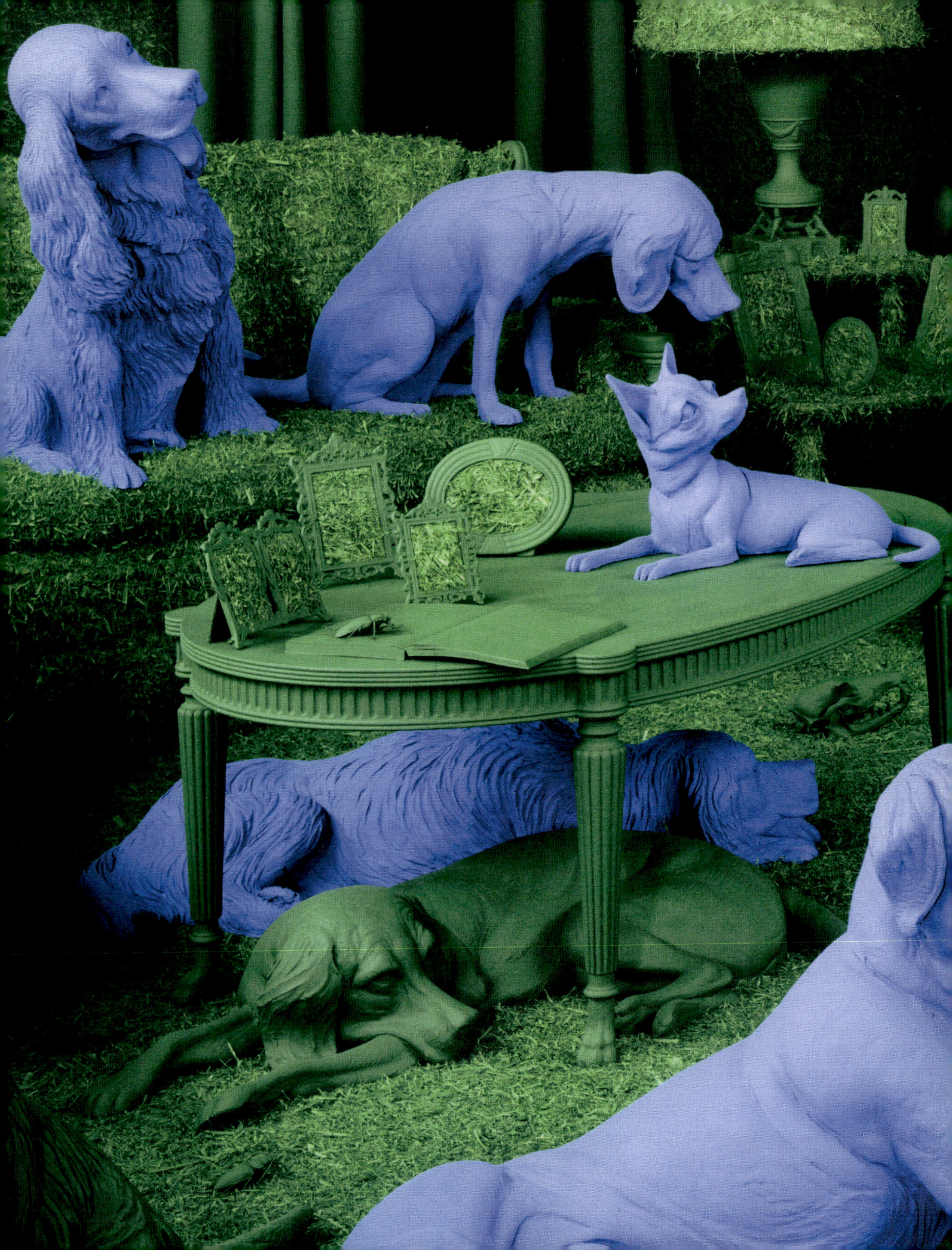

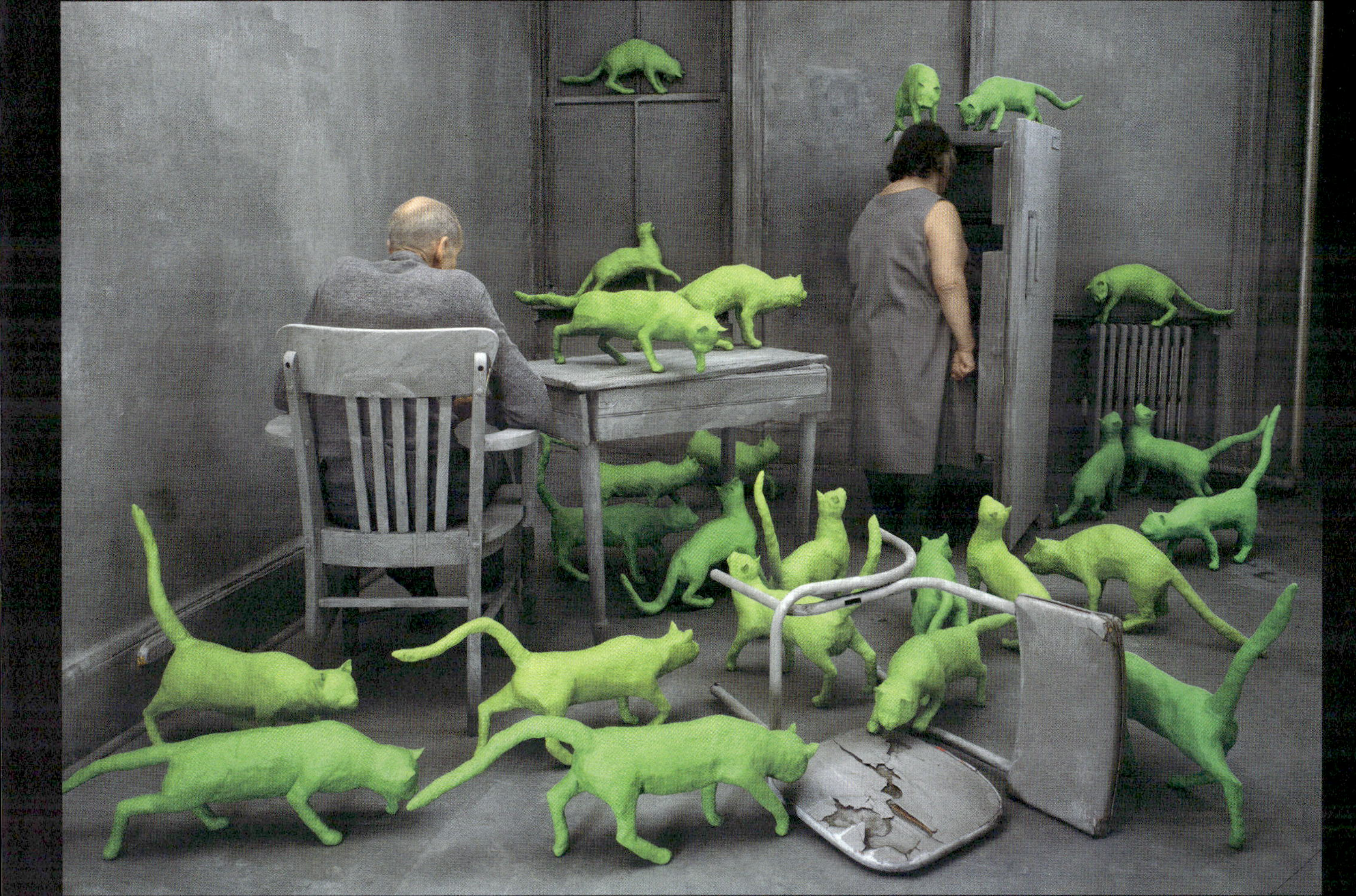

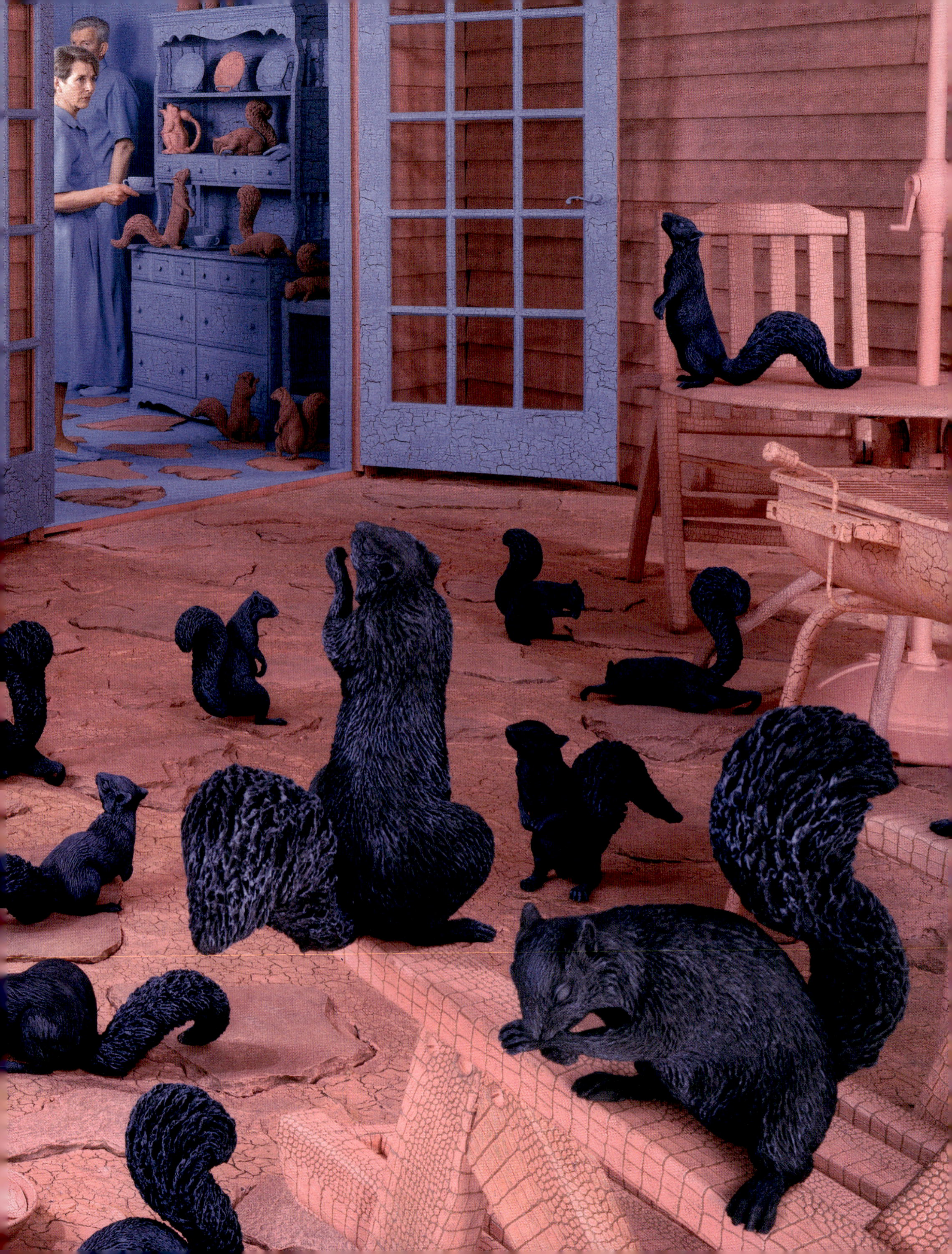

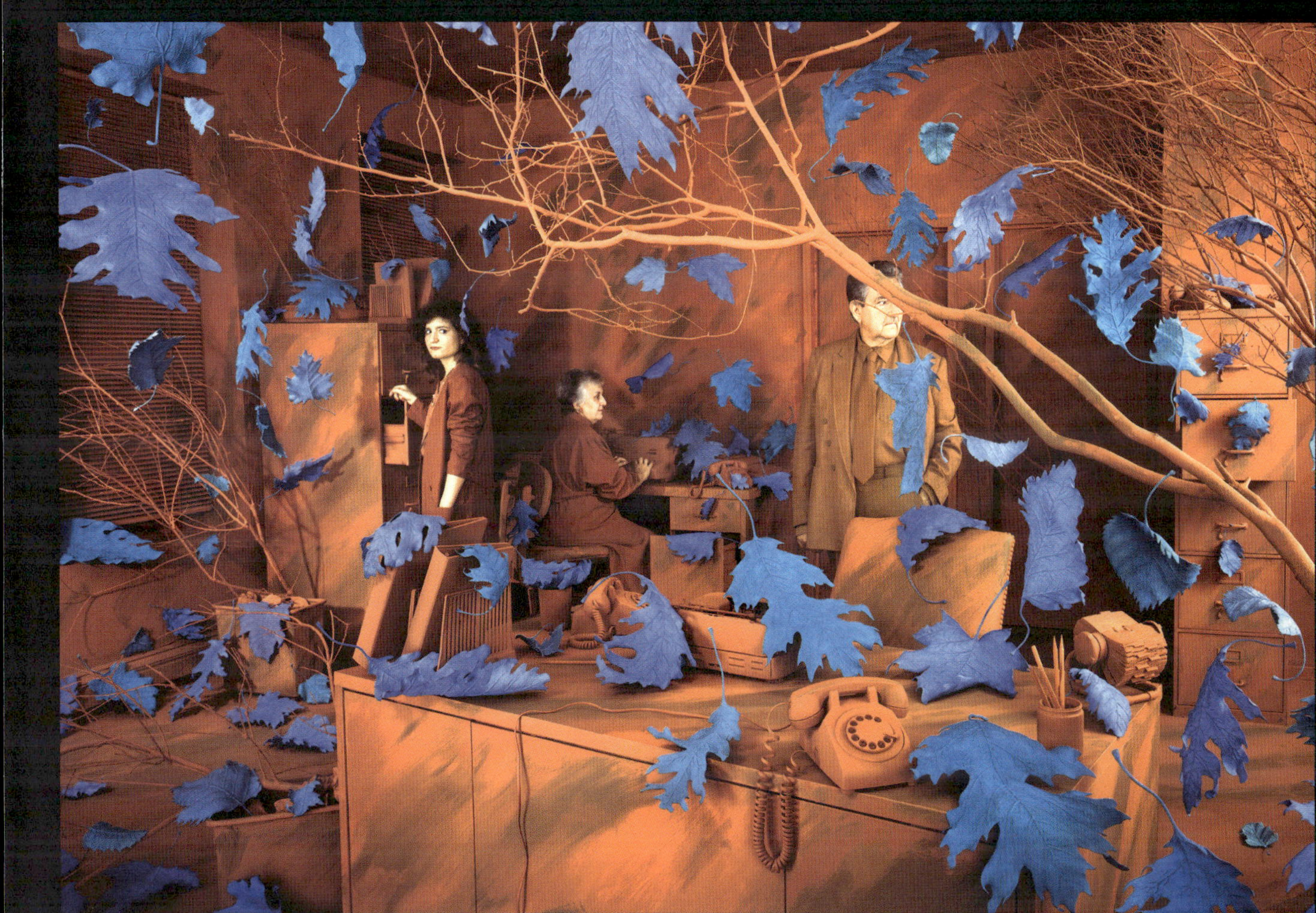

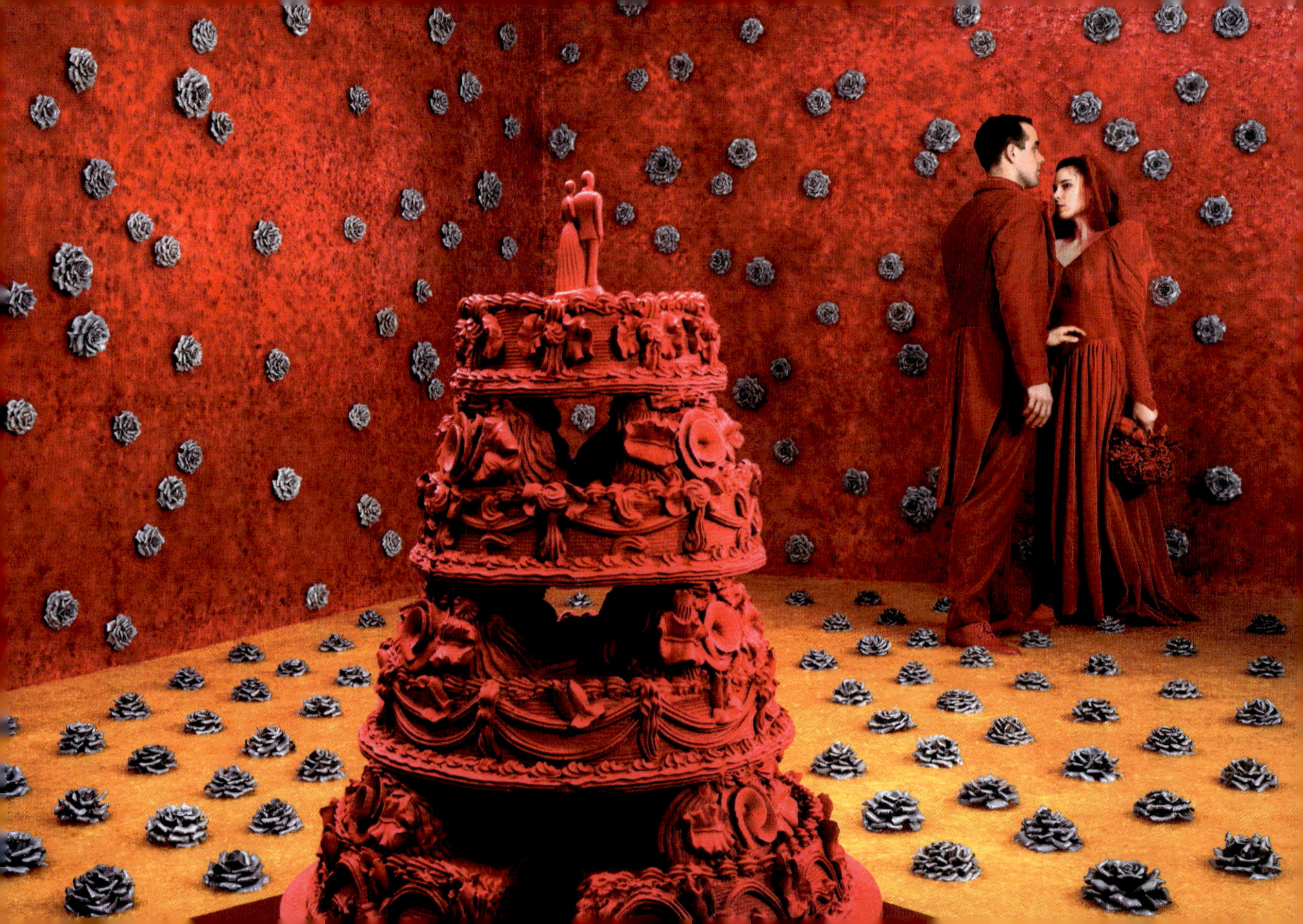

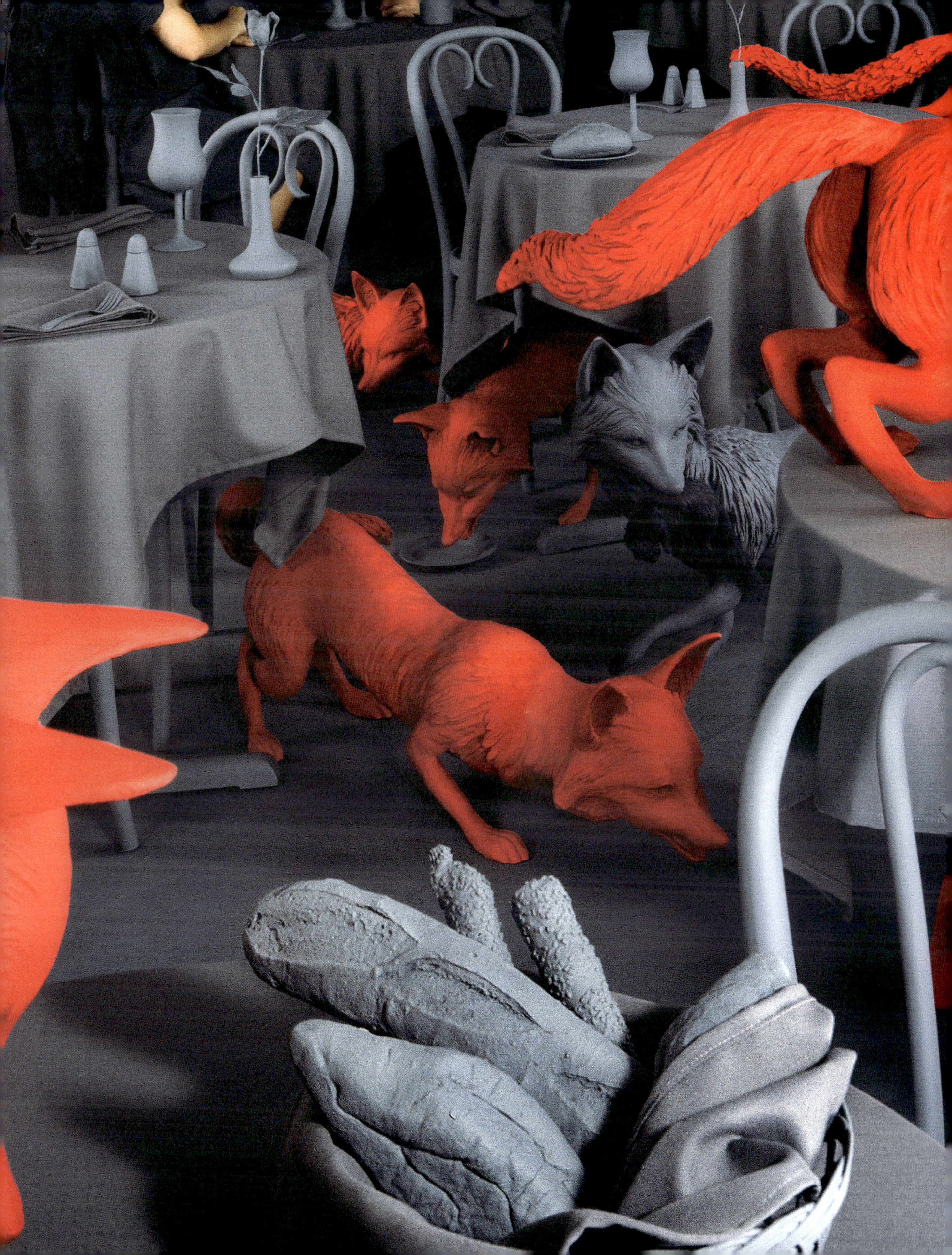

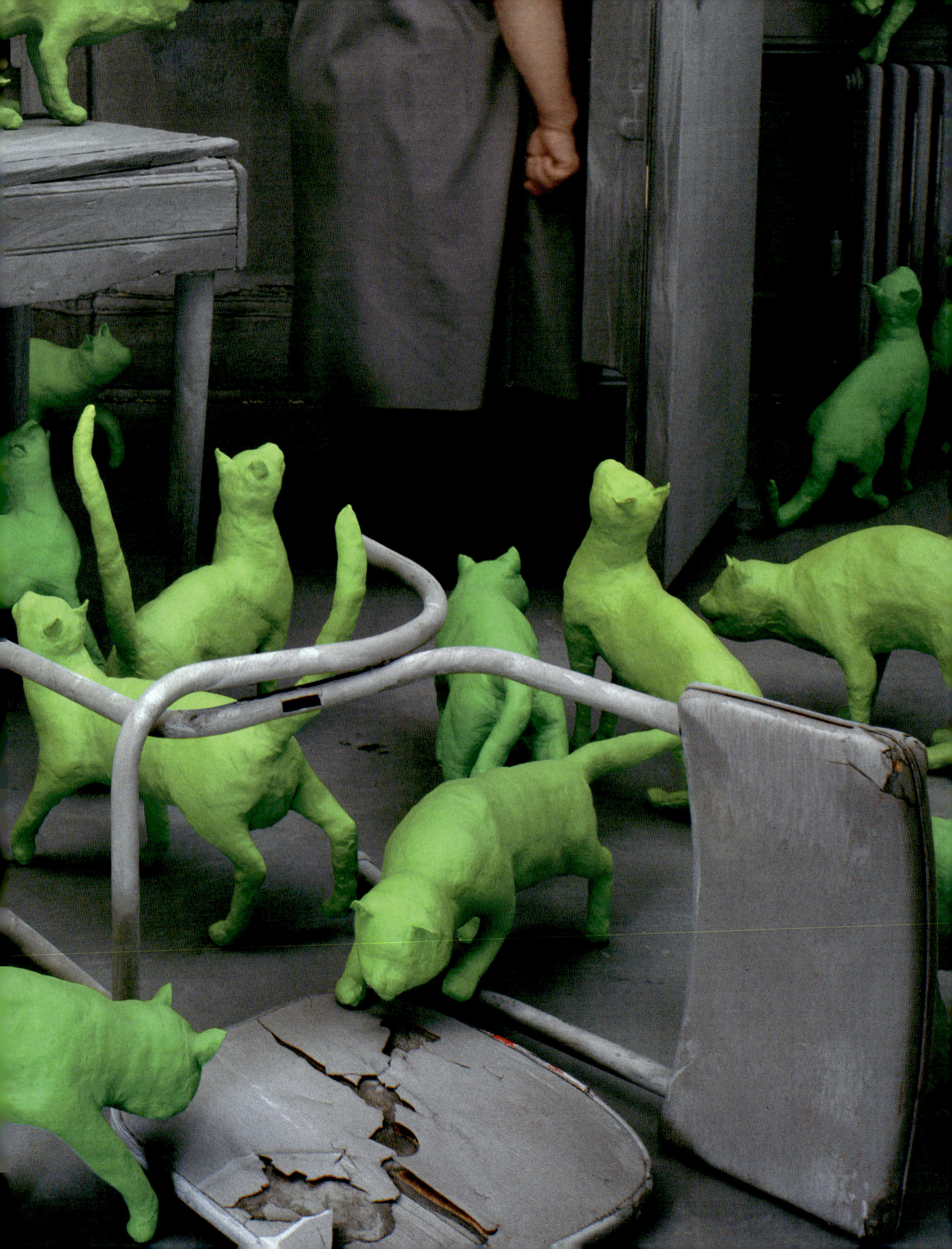

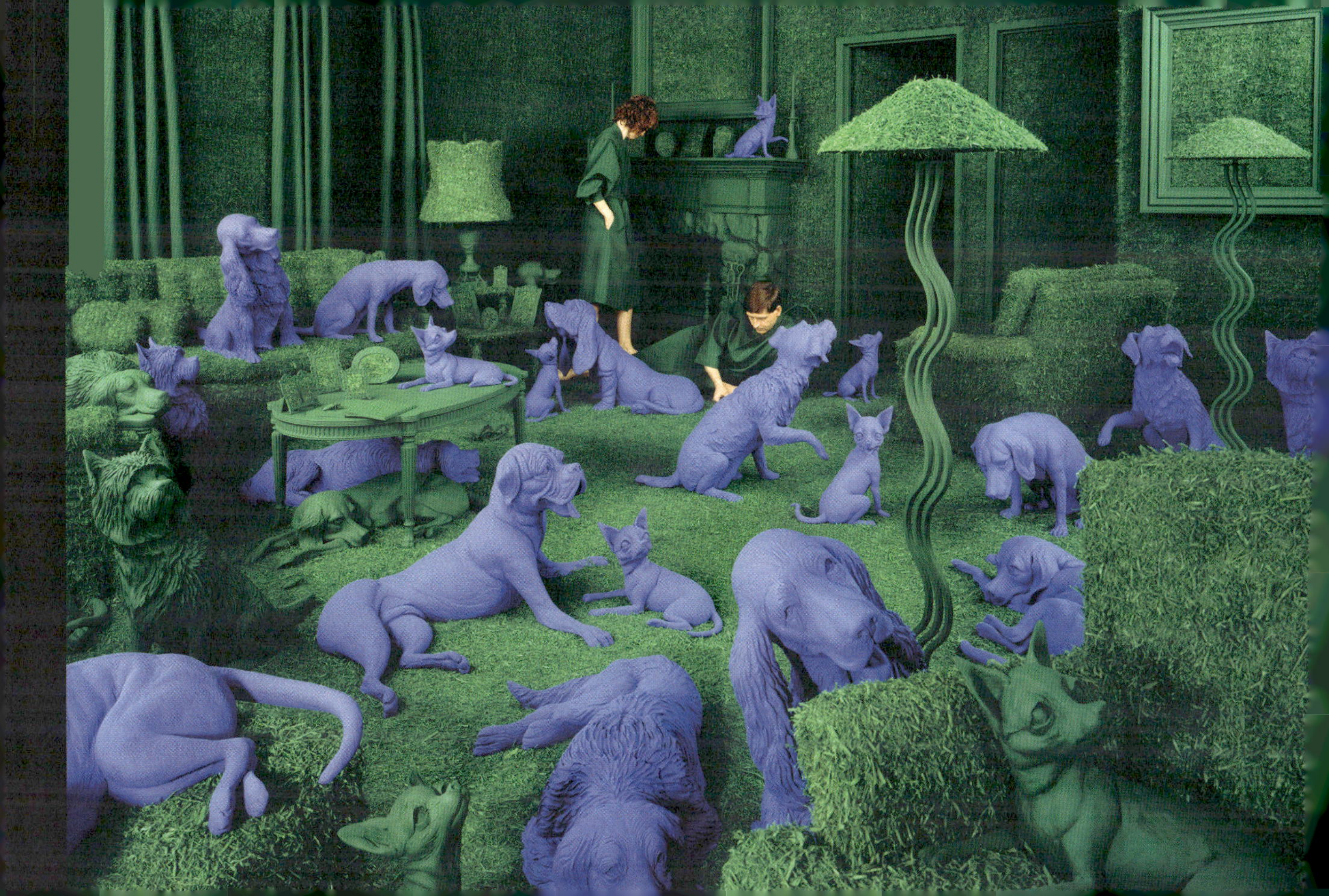

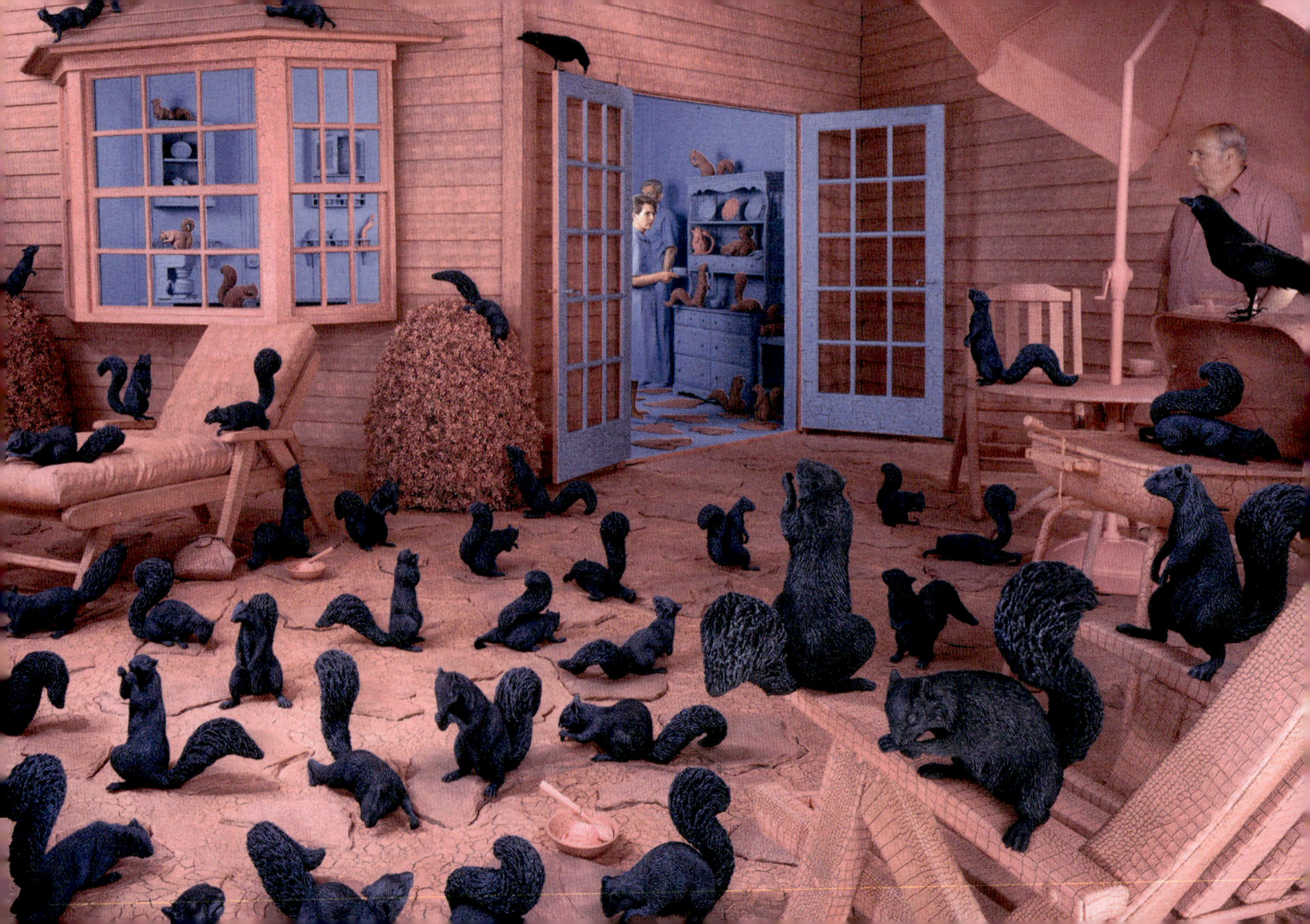

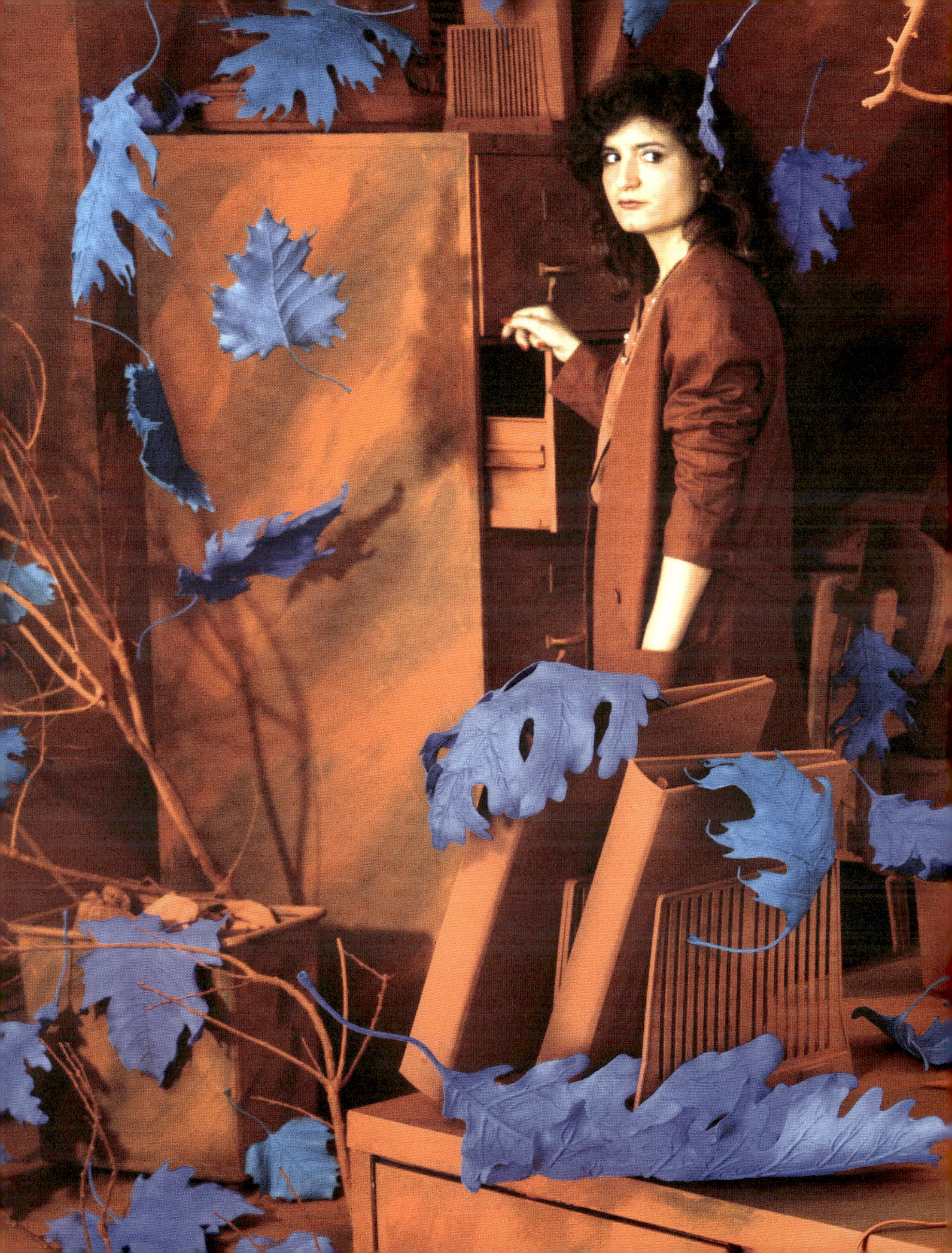

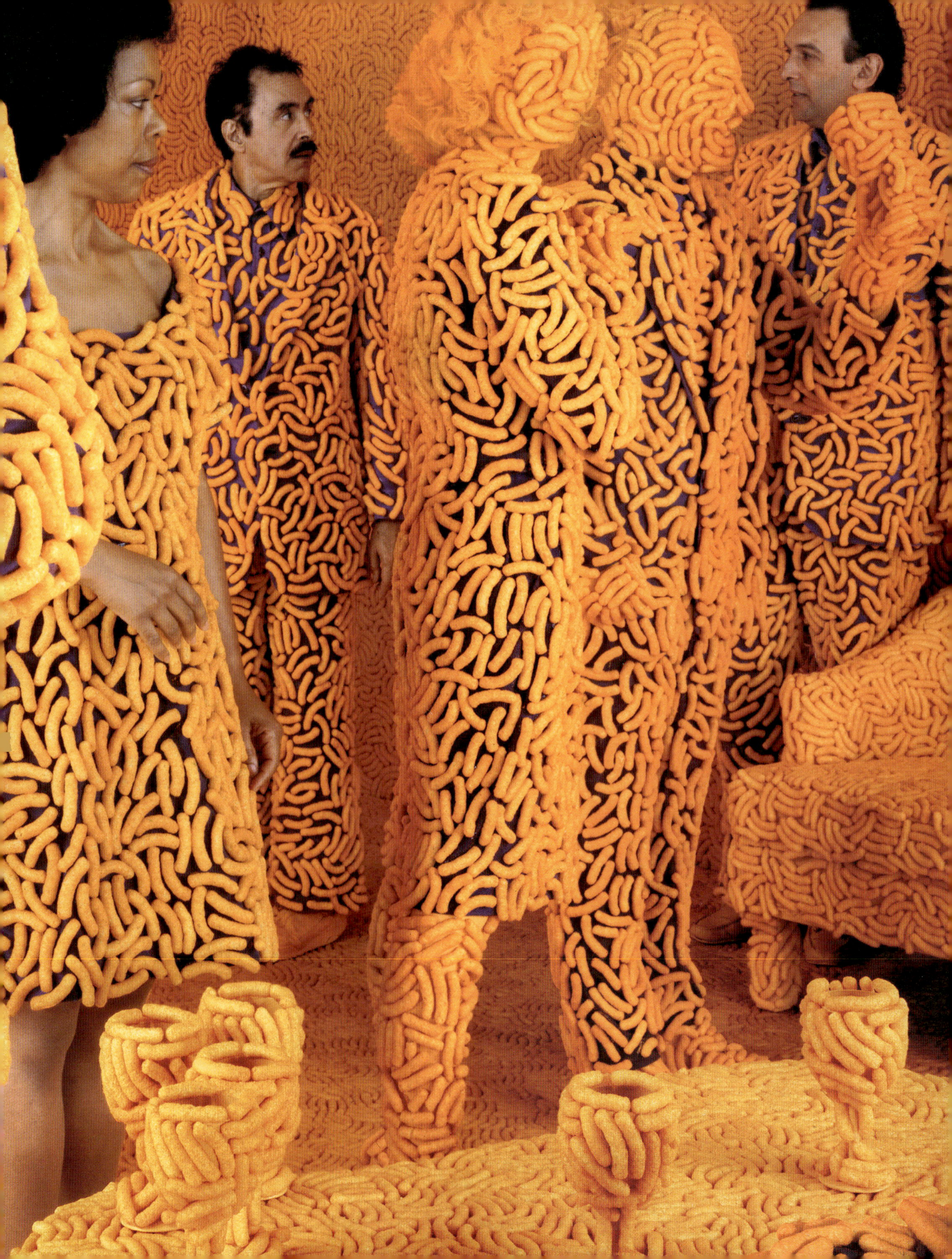

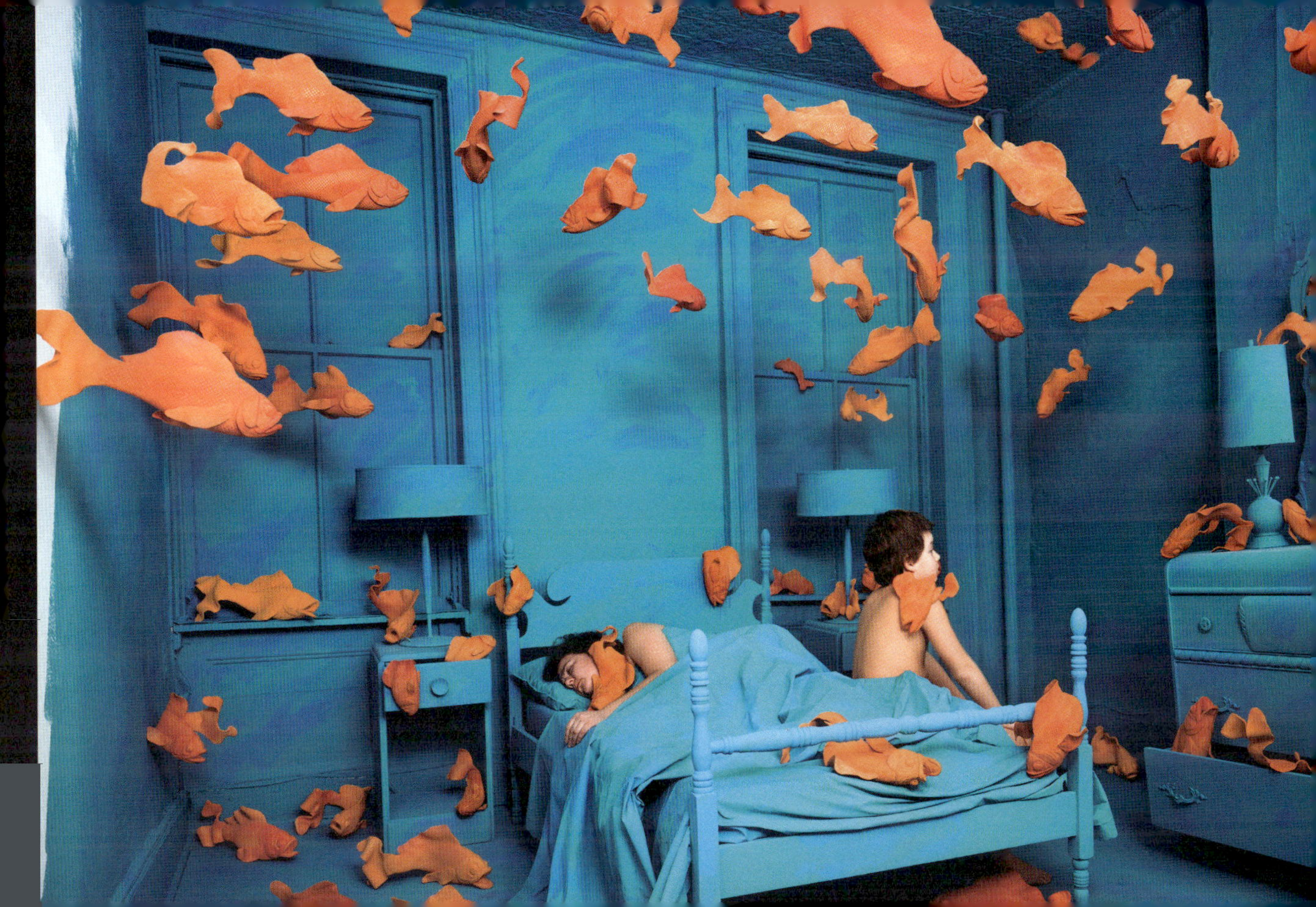

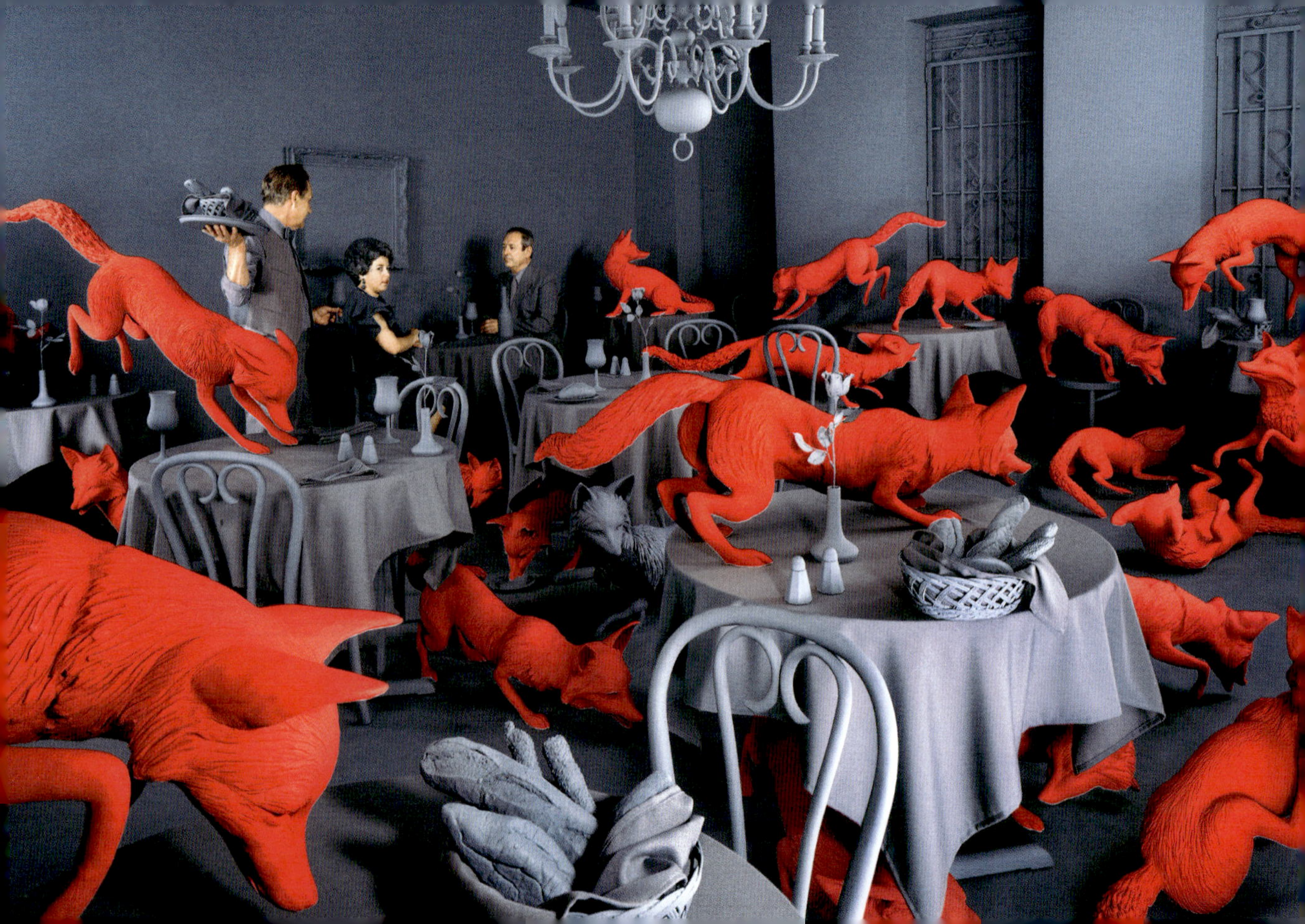

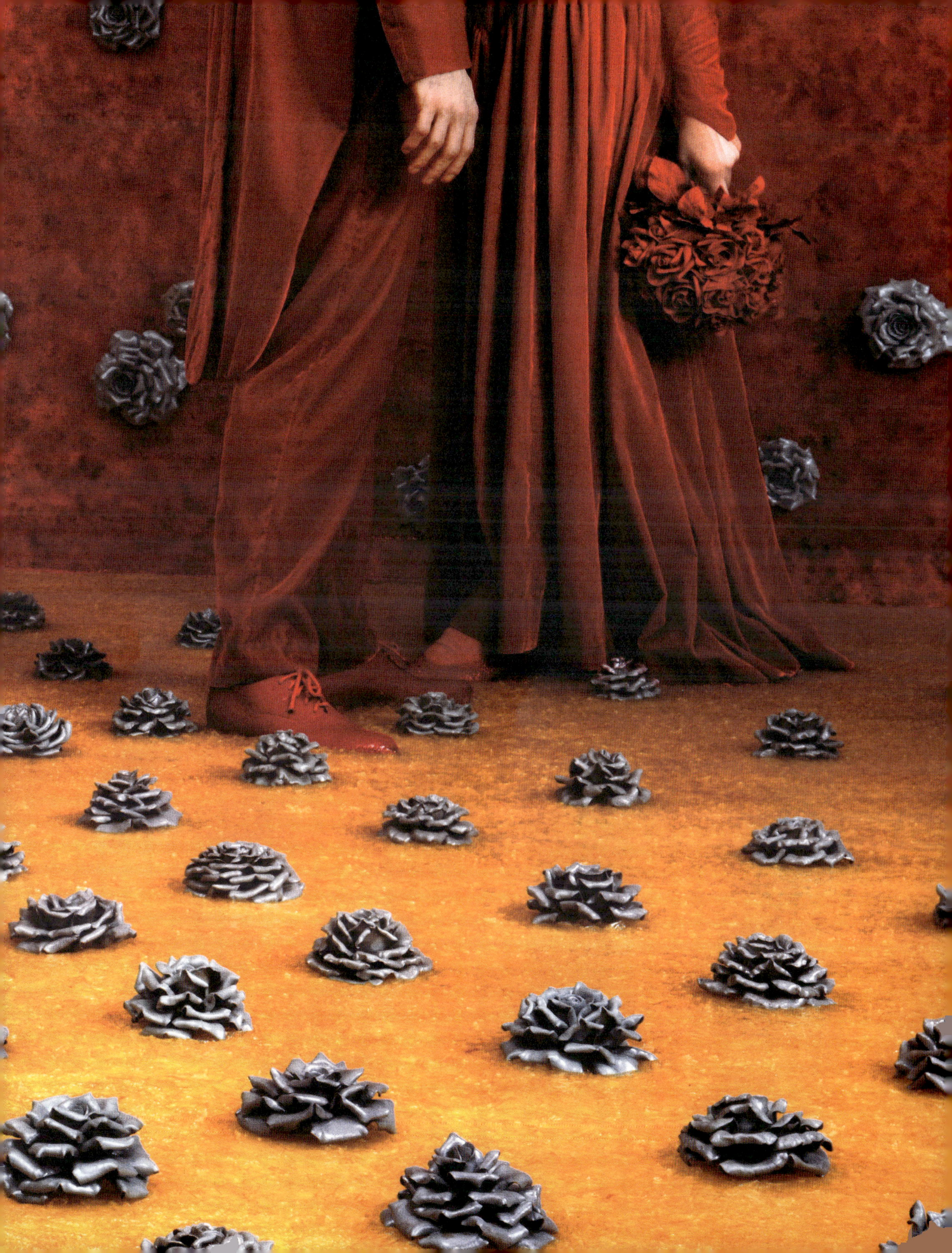

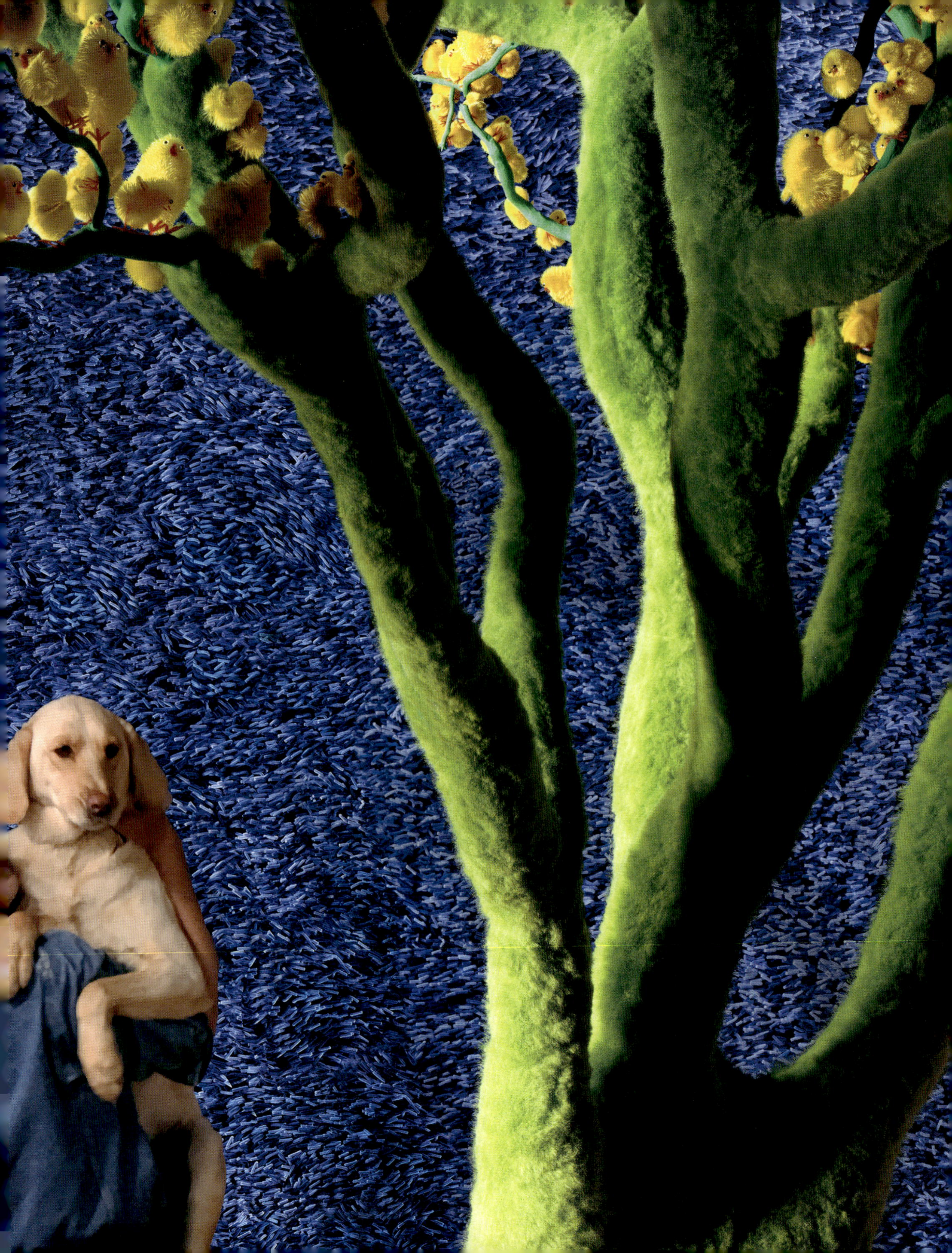

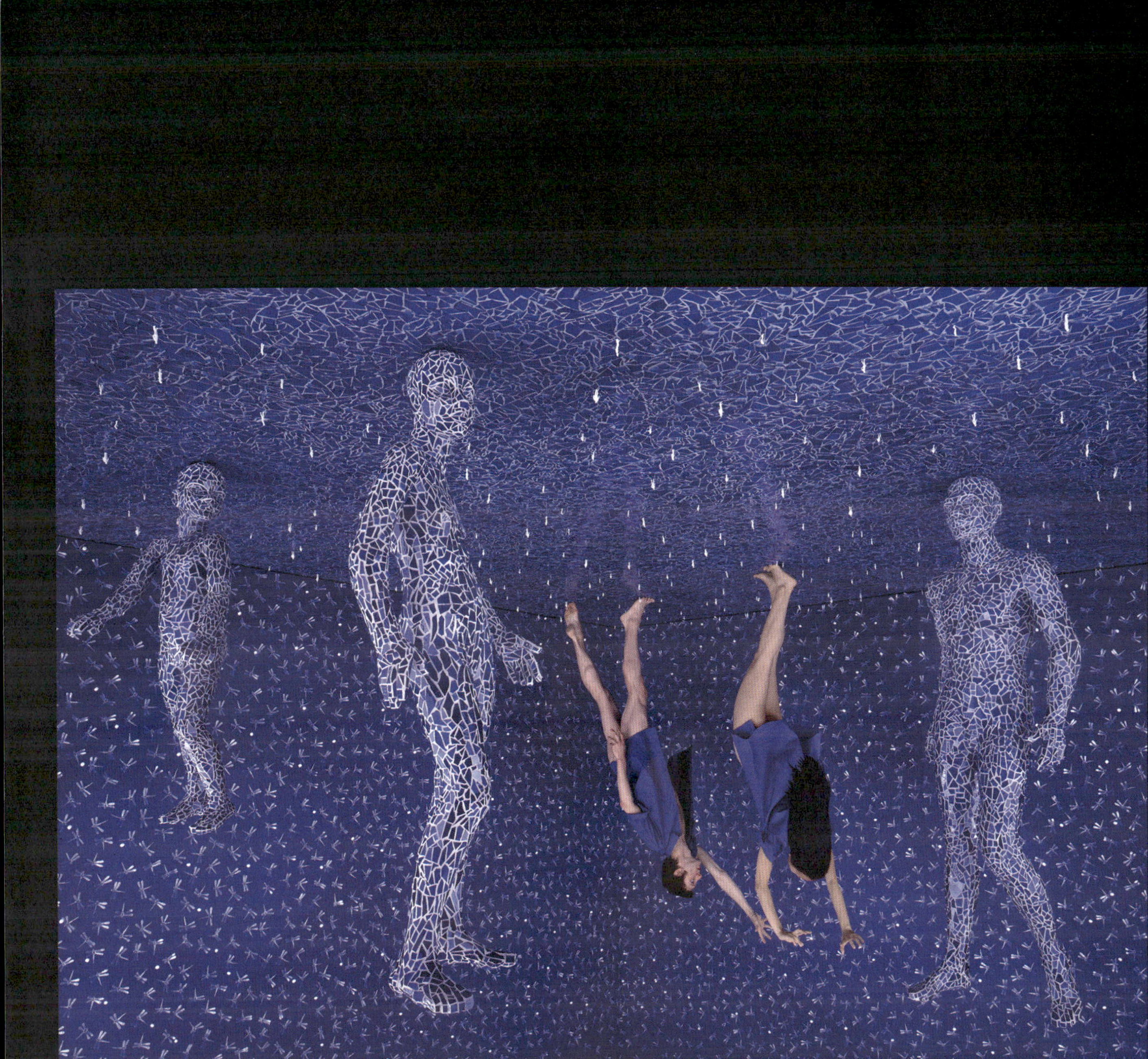

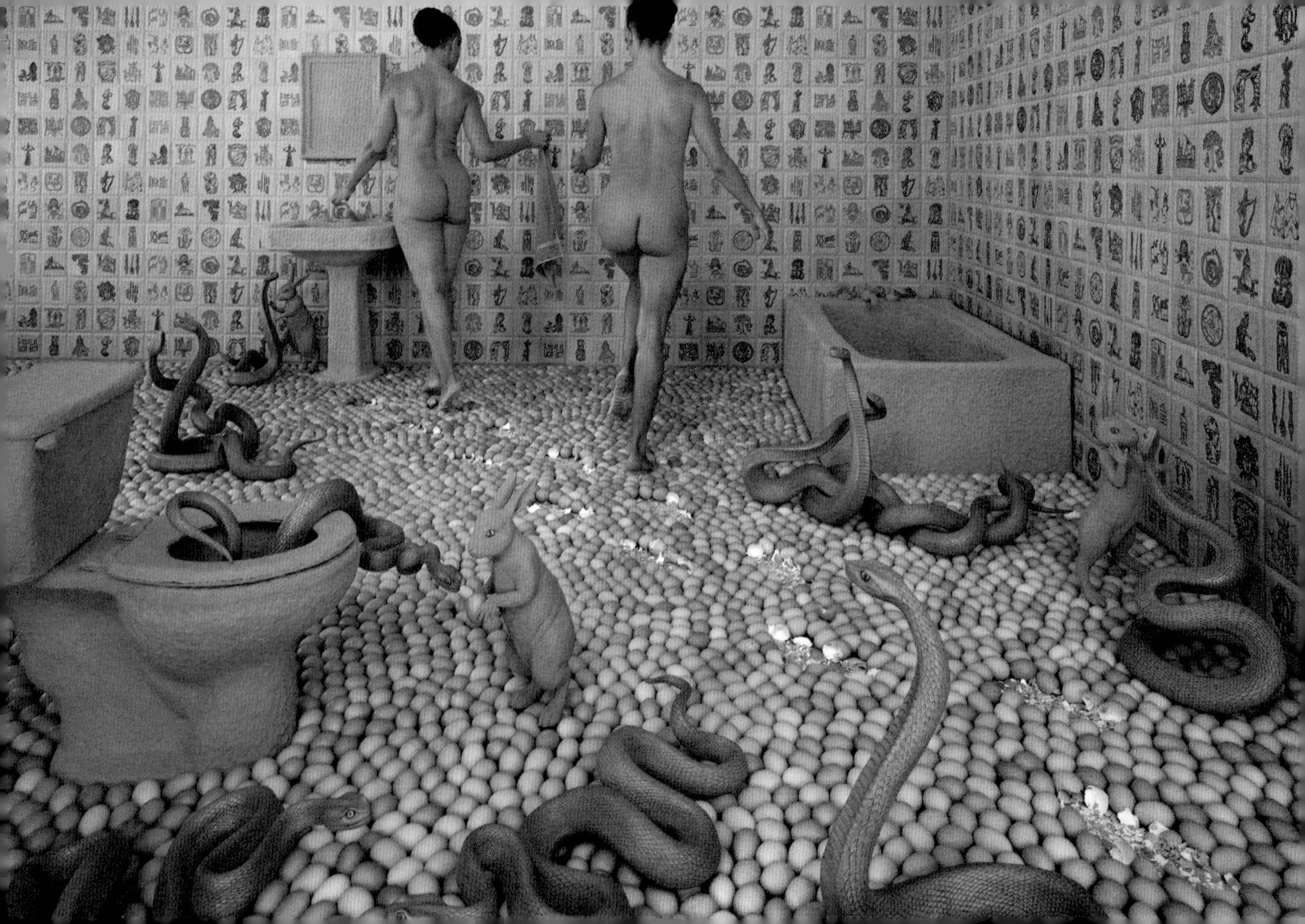

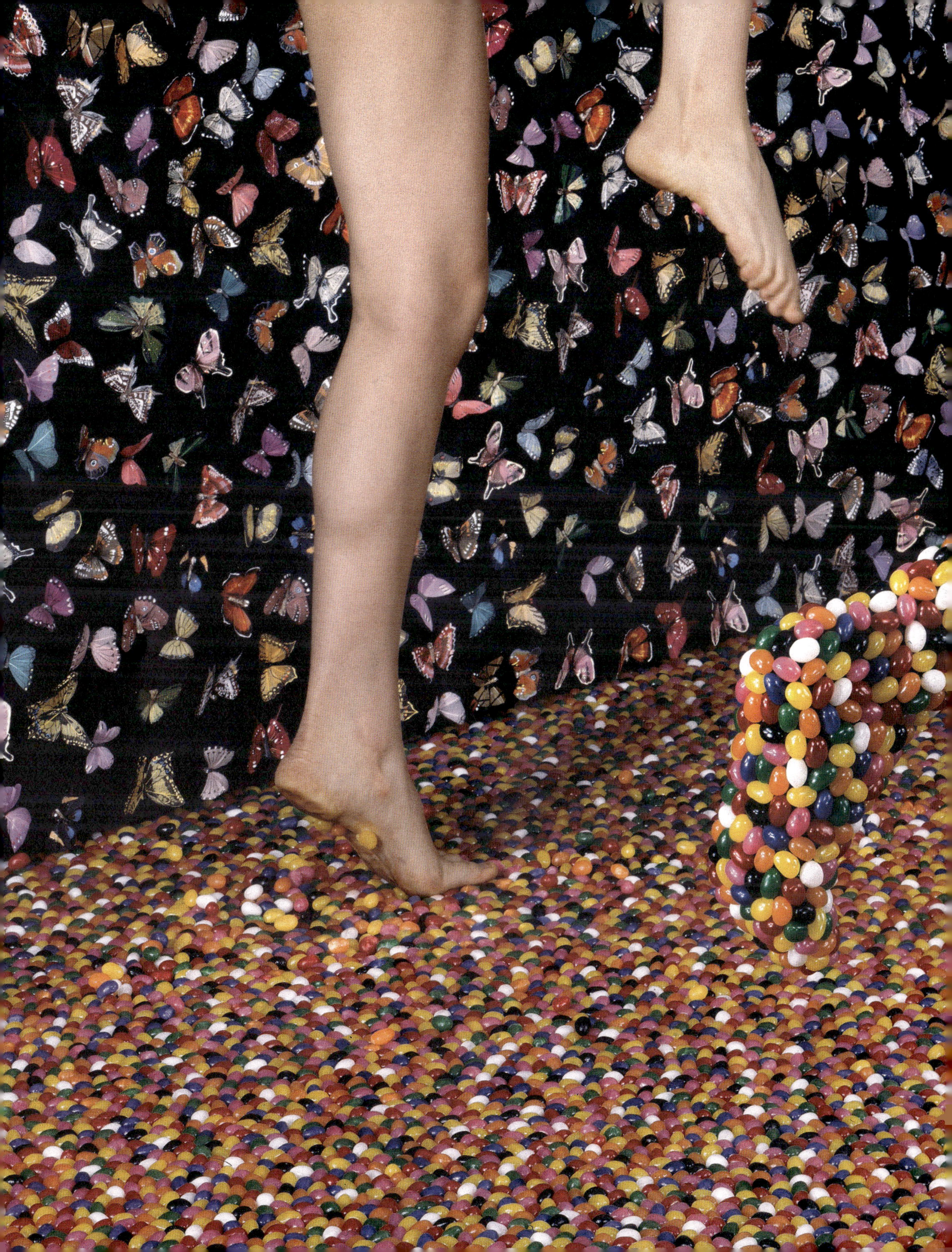

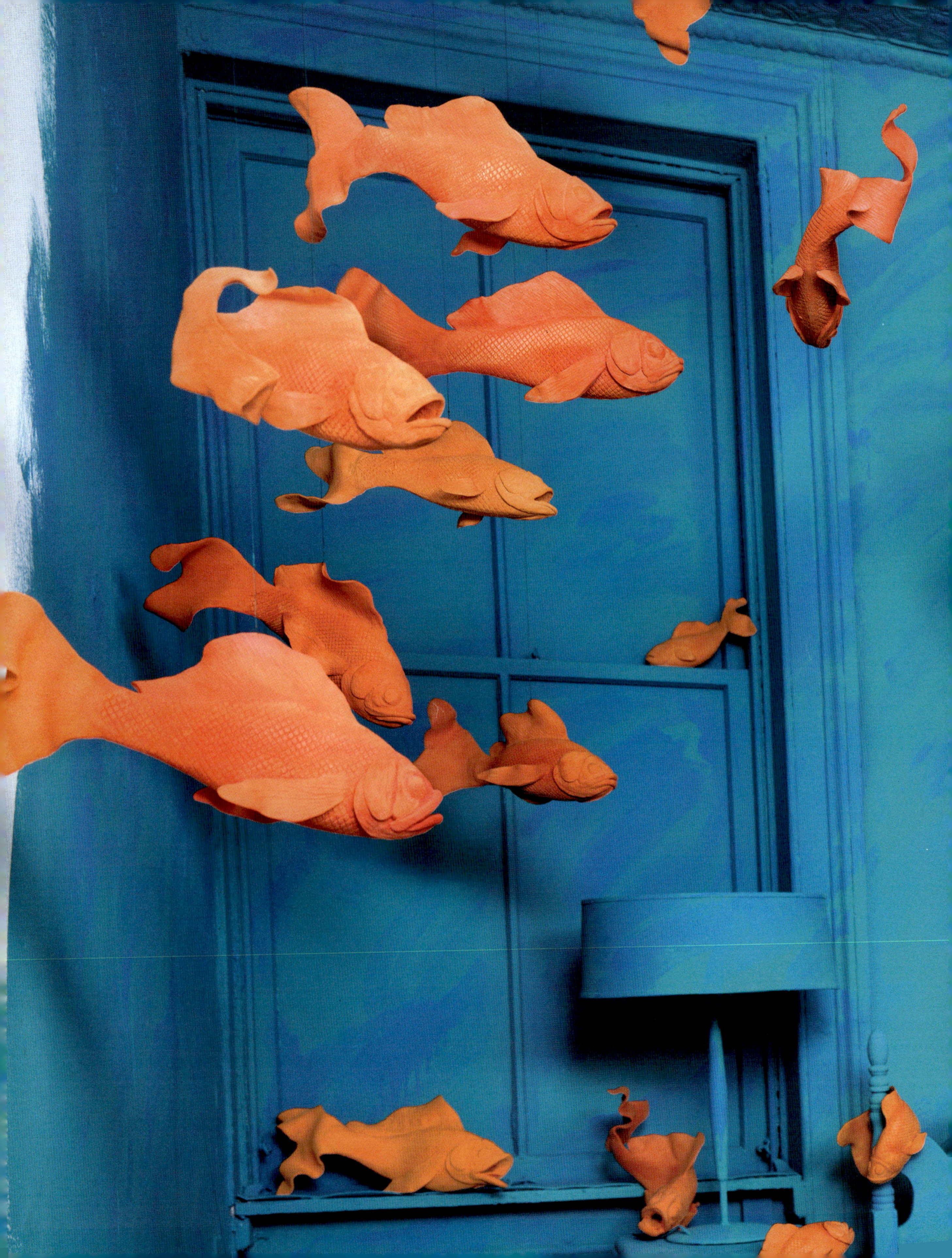

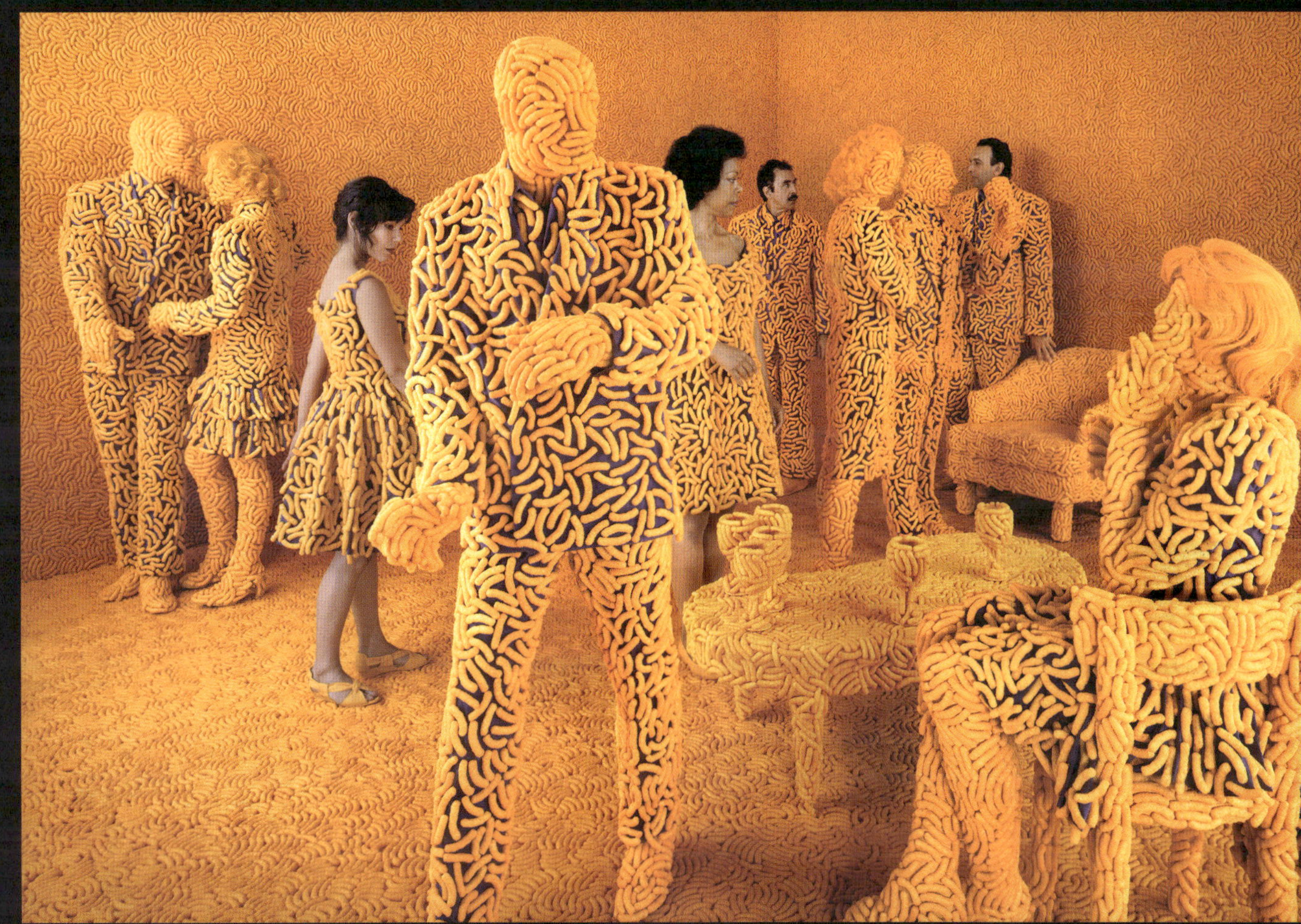

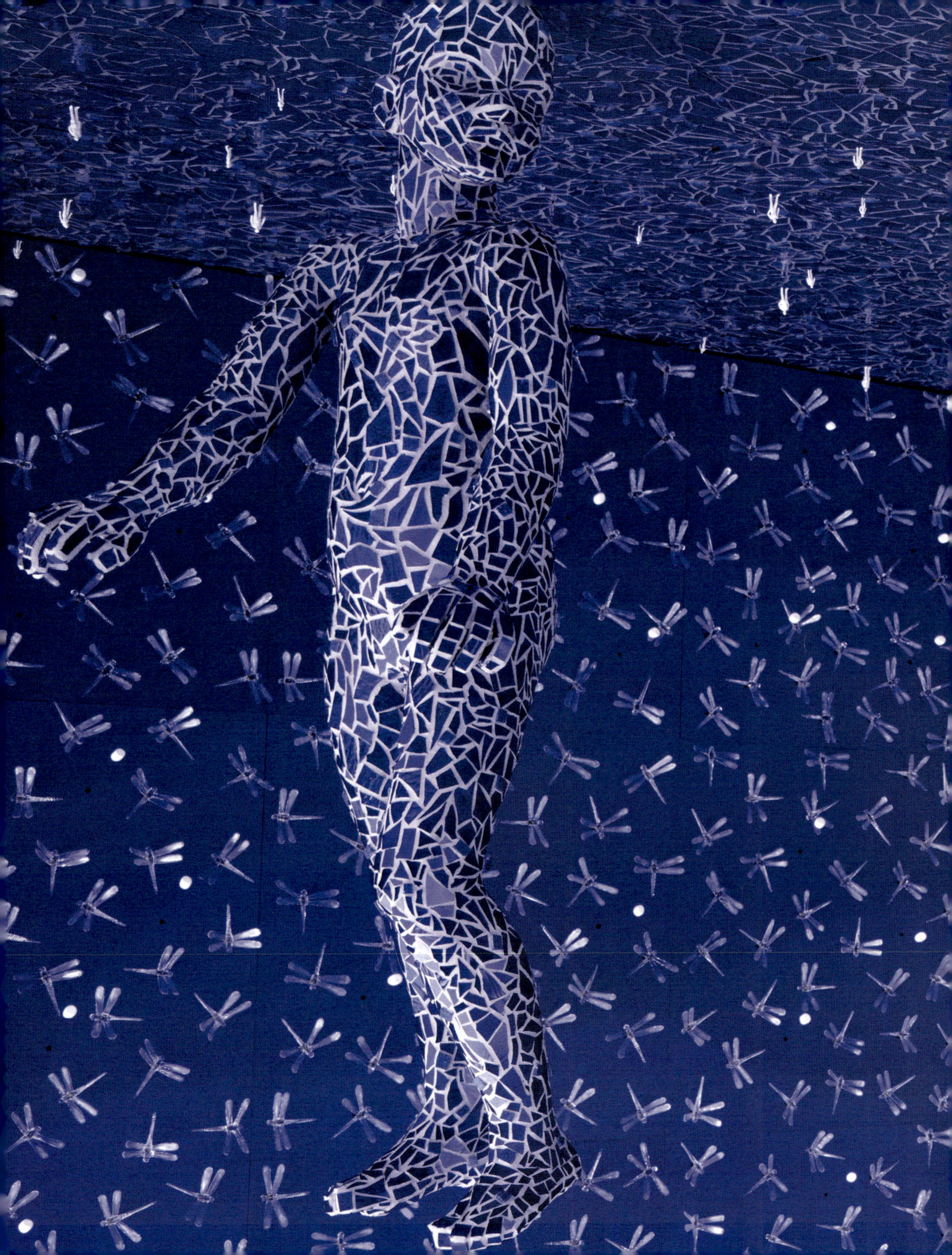

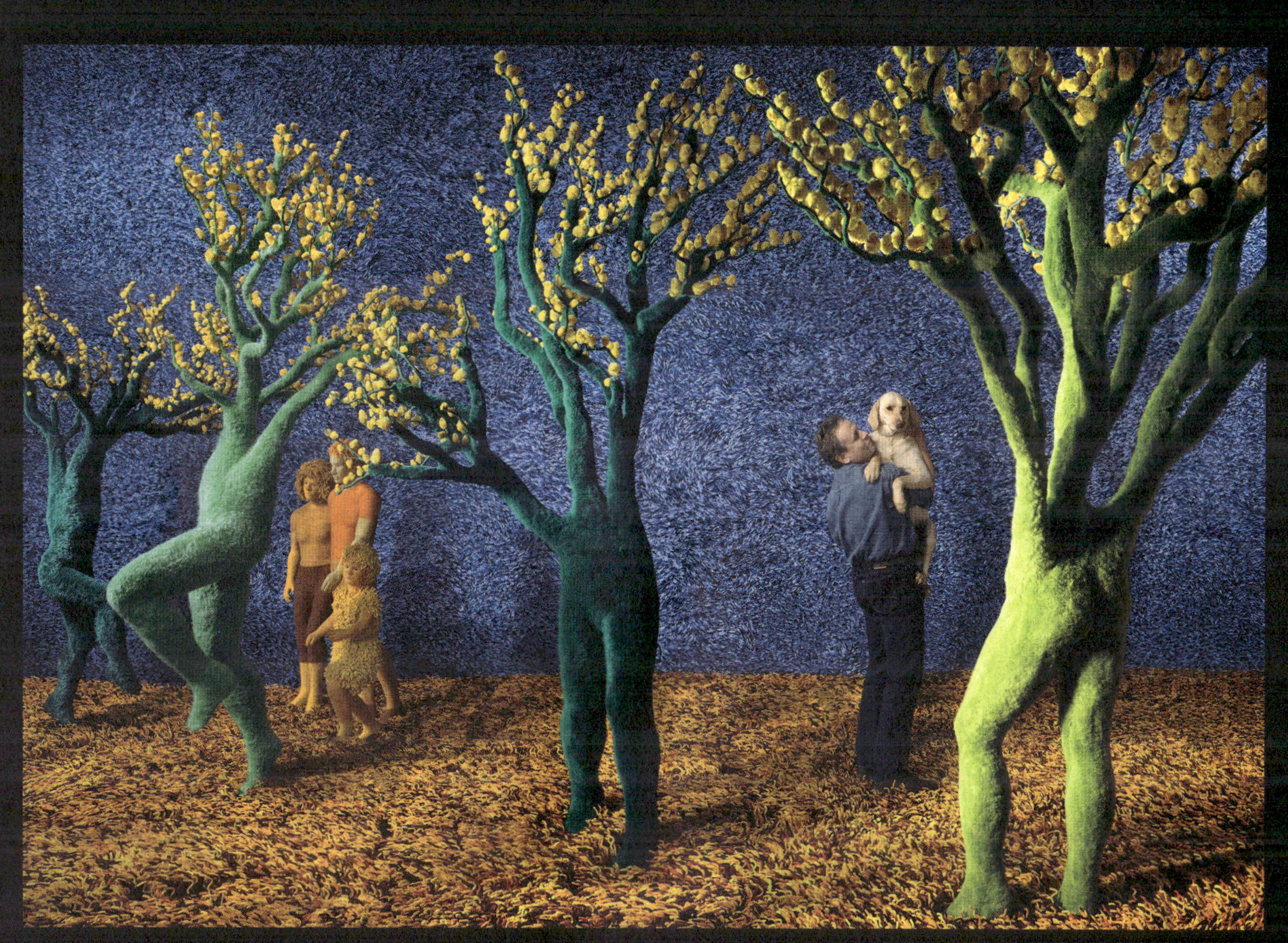

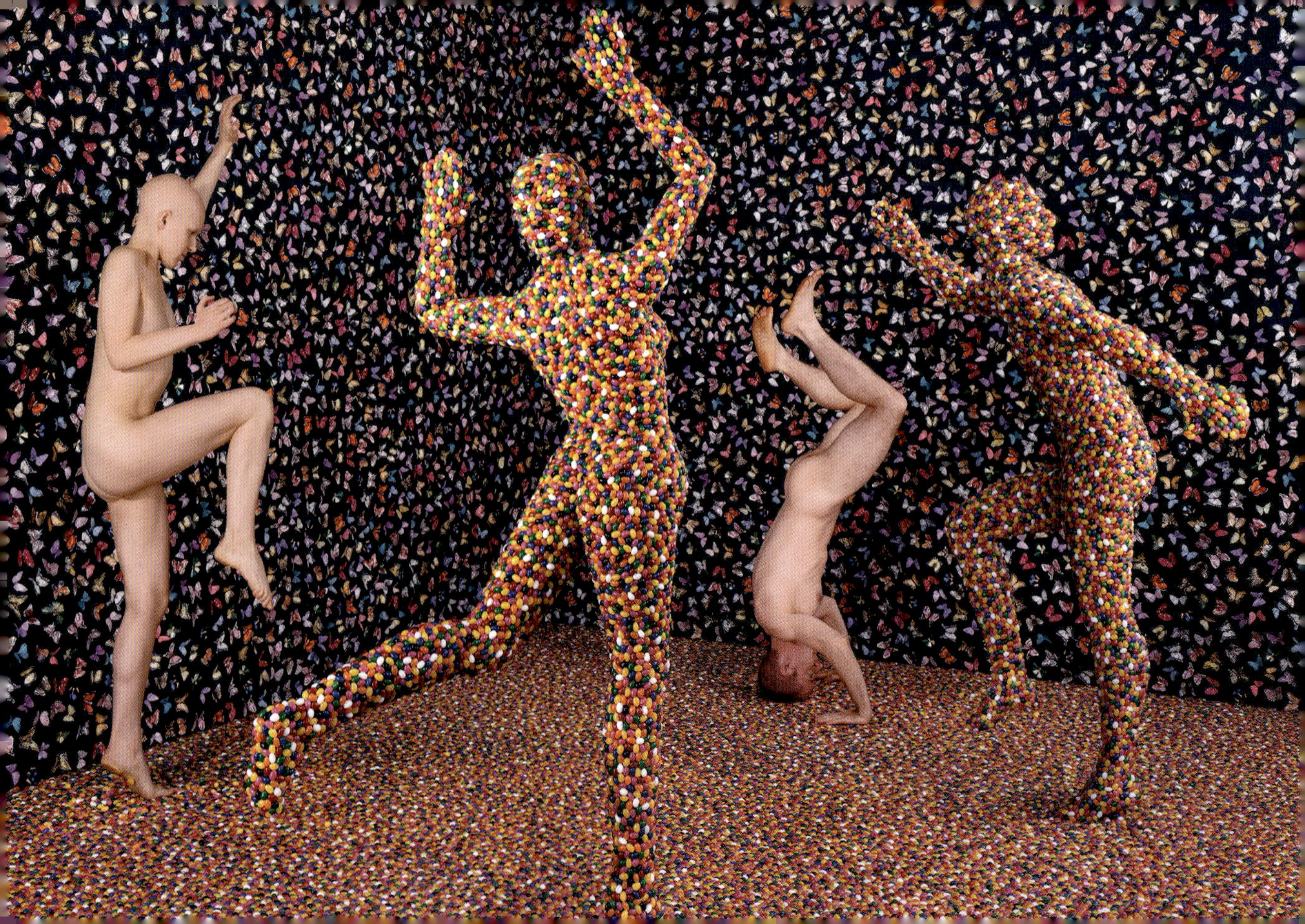

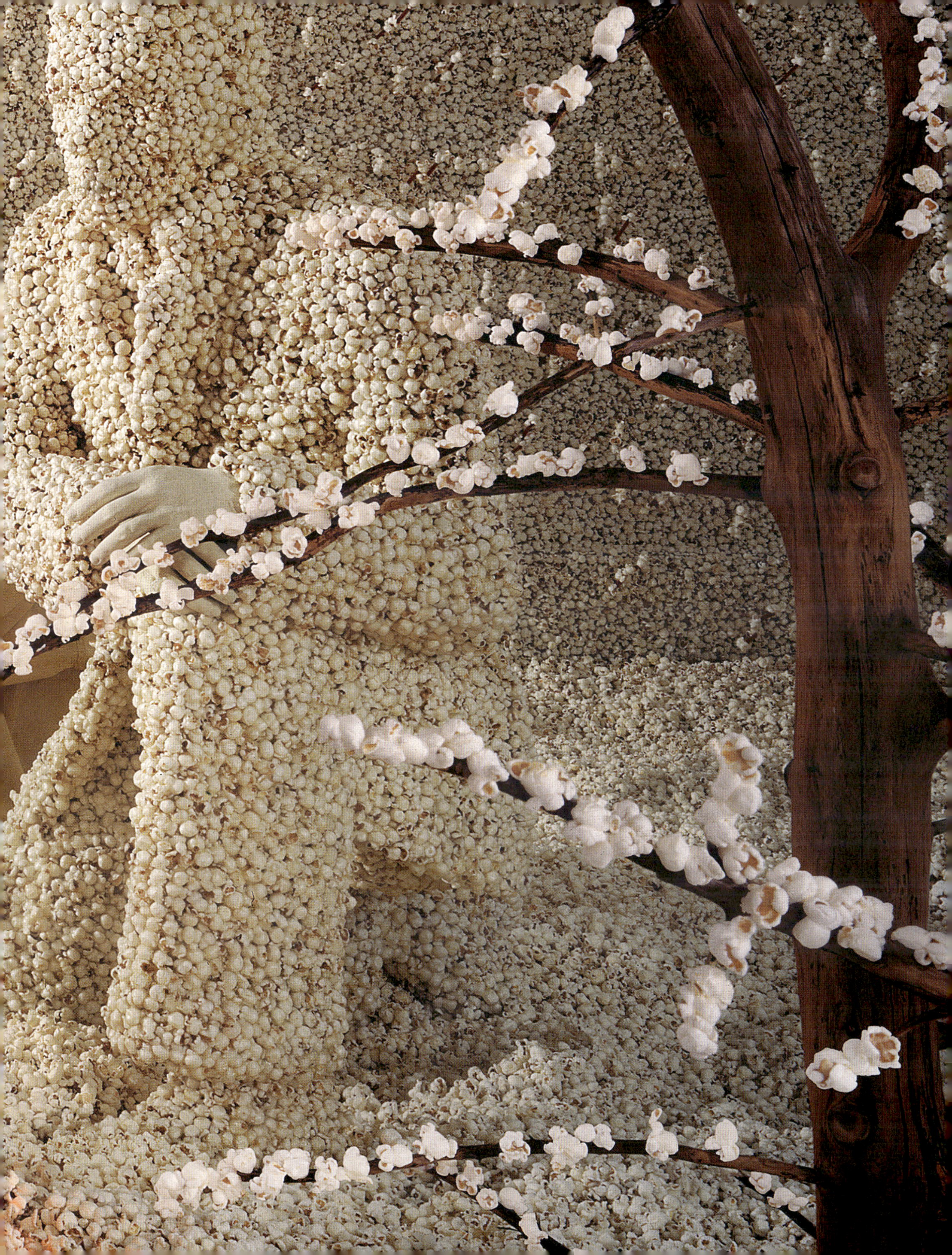

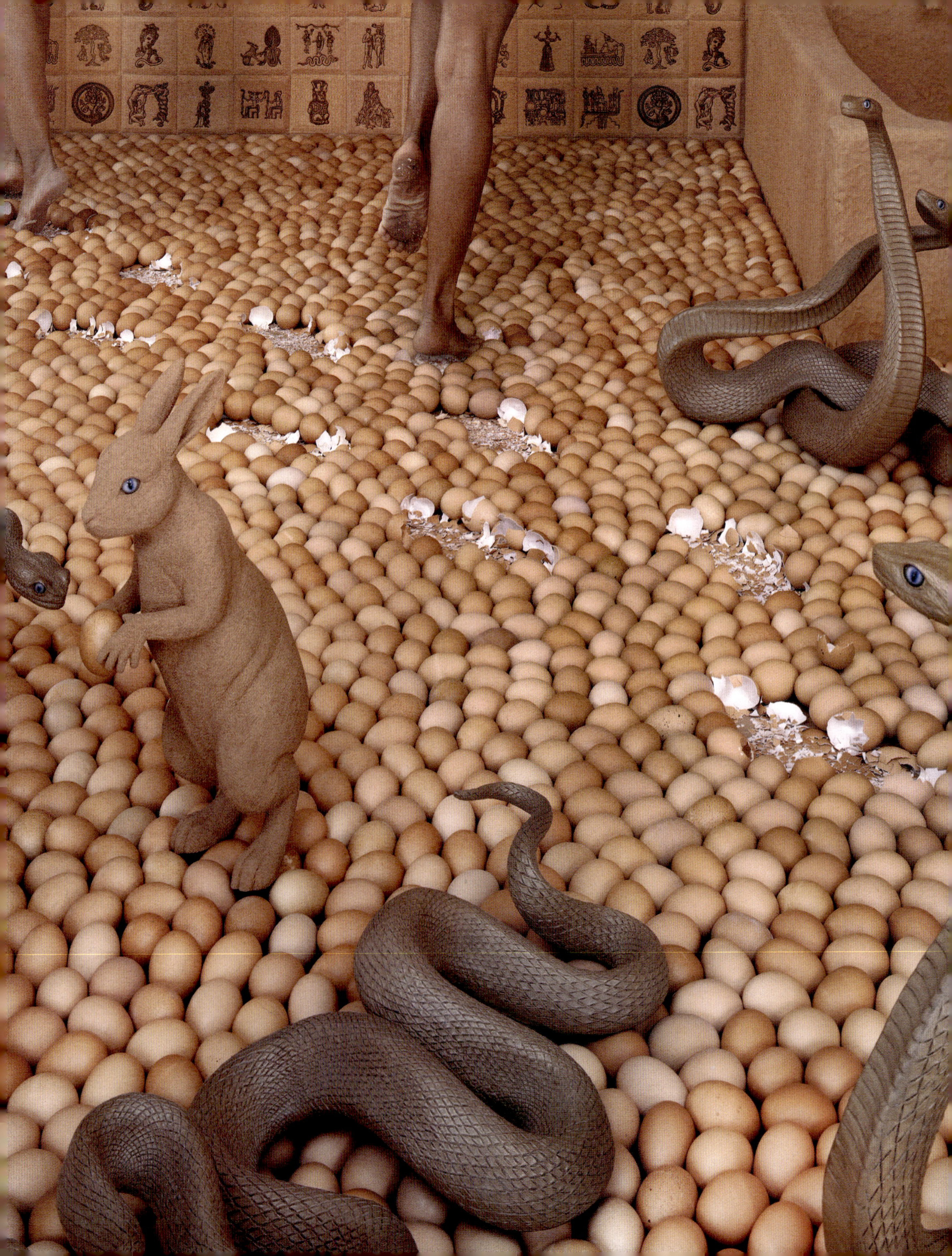

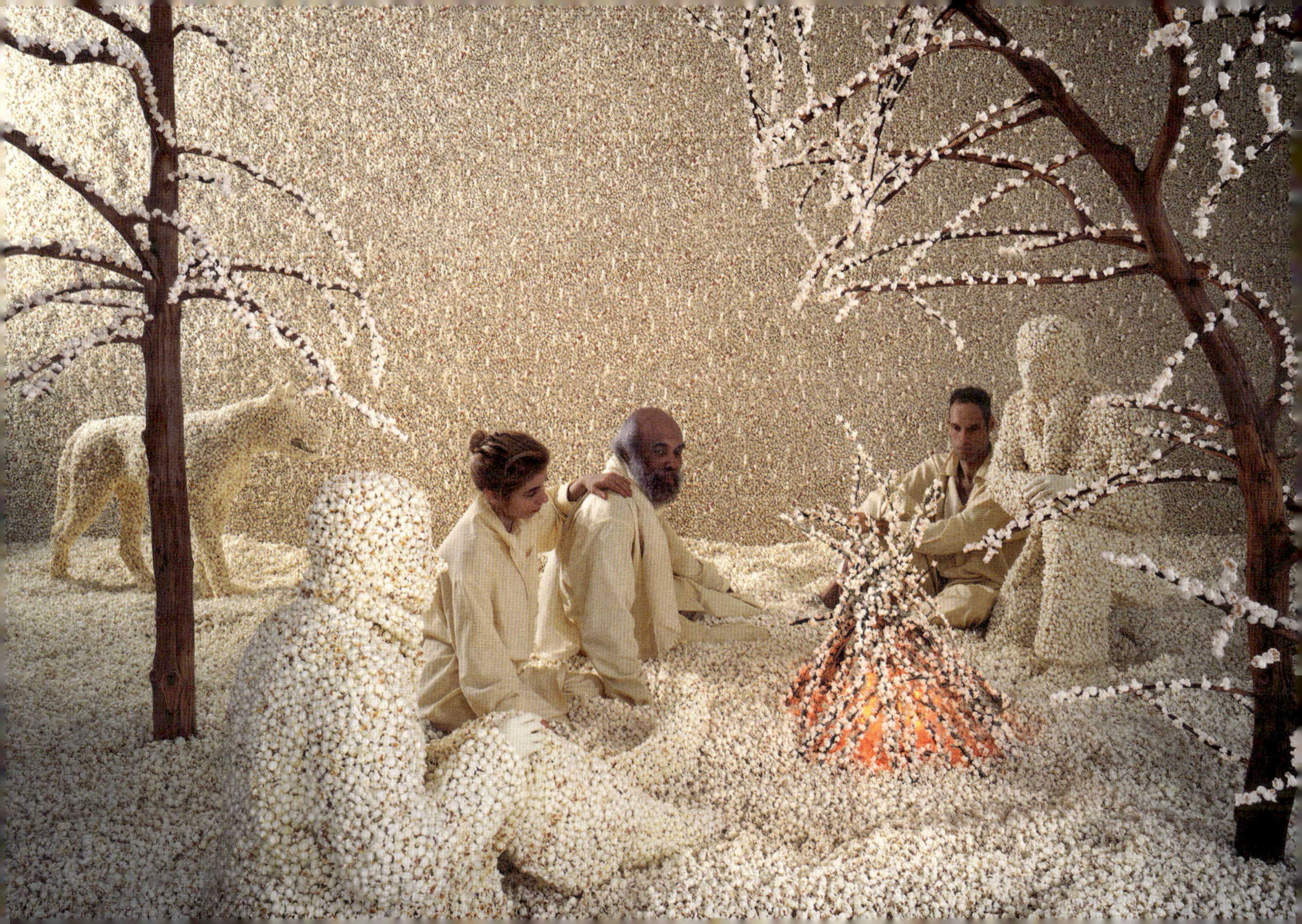

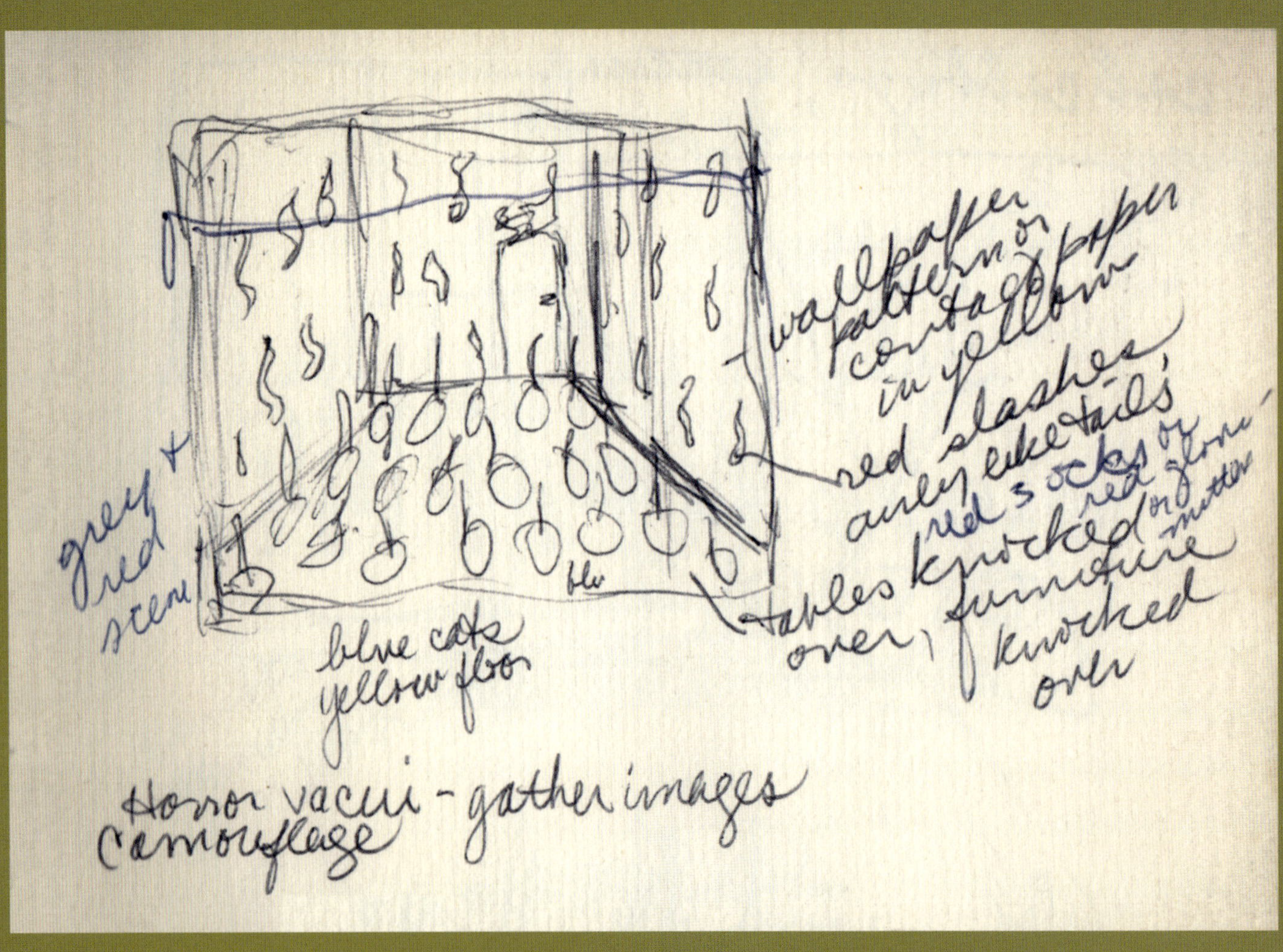

grey +
red
scent
blue cats
yellow floor
blu
wallpaper
pattern or
contact paper
in yellow
red slashes,
curly like tails
red socks or
red glove
tables knocked
over, furniture
butter
knocked
over
Horror vacui - gather images
camouflage

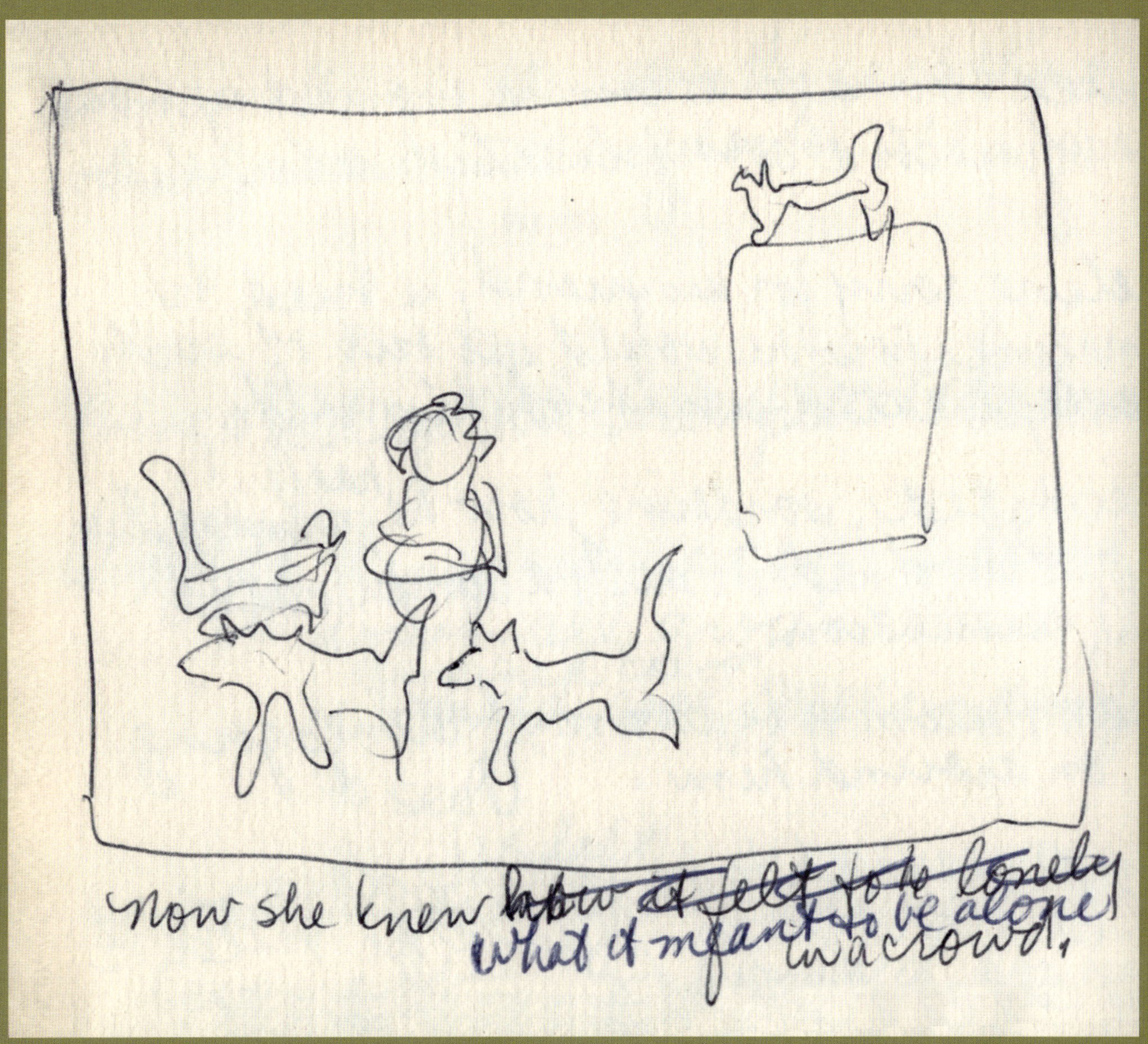

now she knew how it felt to be lonely what it meant to be alone in a crowd.

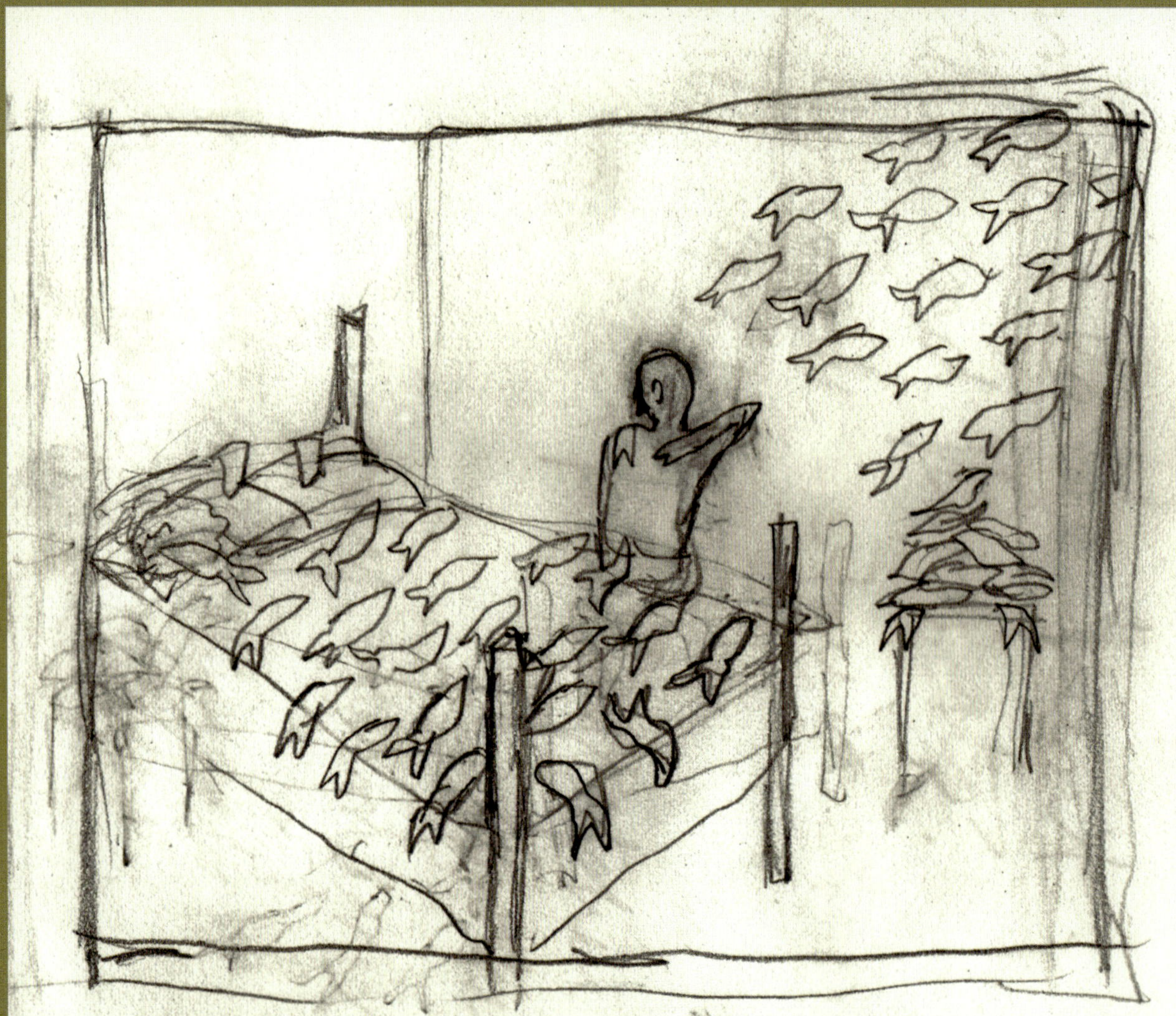

TWO KINDS OF FISH
BREAKING AWAY

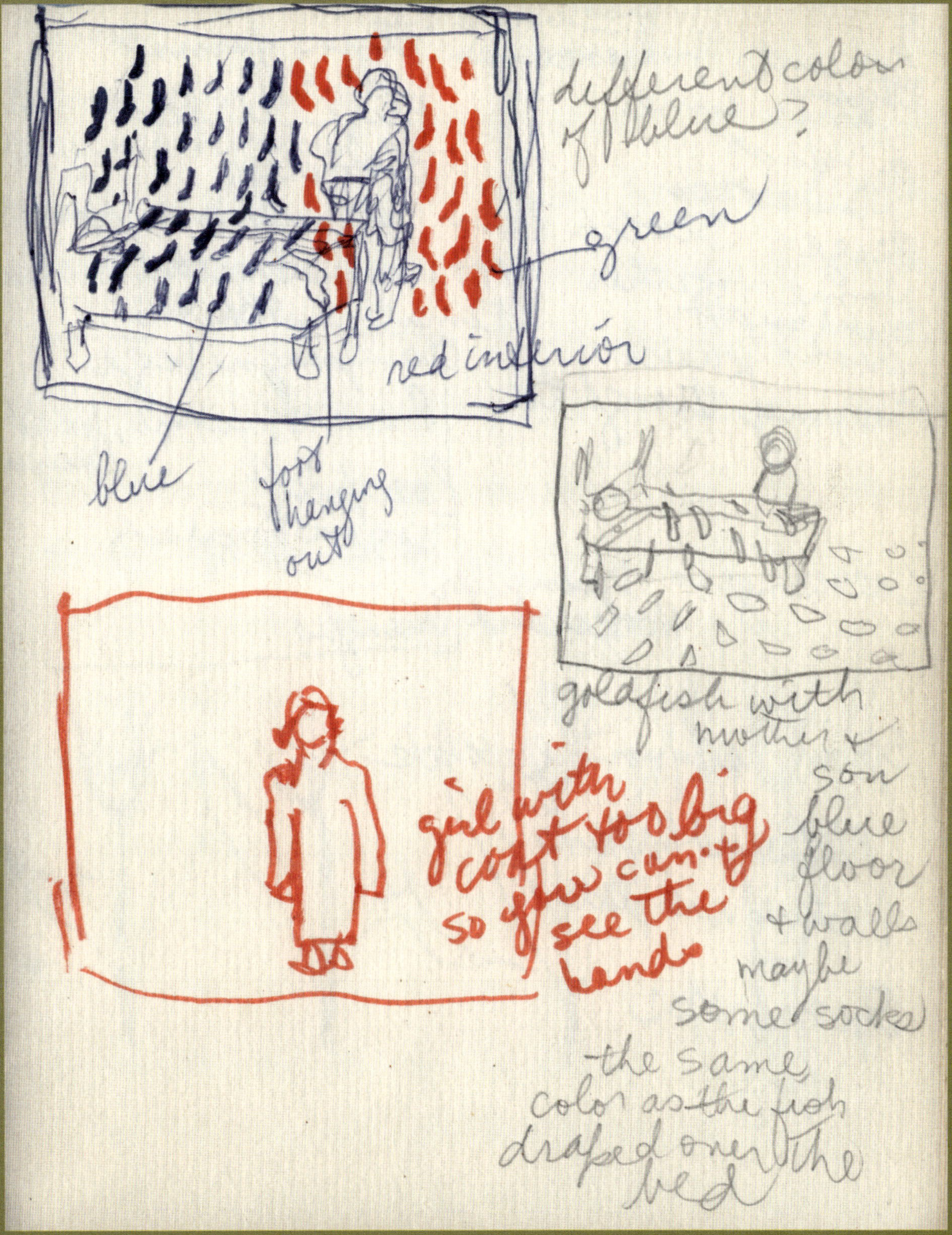

different colour
of blue?

green

red interior

blue

foot
hanging
out

girl with
coat too big
so you can't
see the
hands

goldfish with
mother &
son
blue
floor
& walls
maybe
some socks
— the same
color as the fish
draped over the
bed

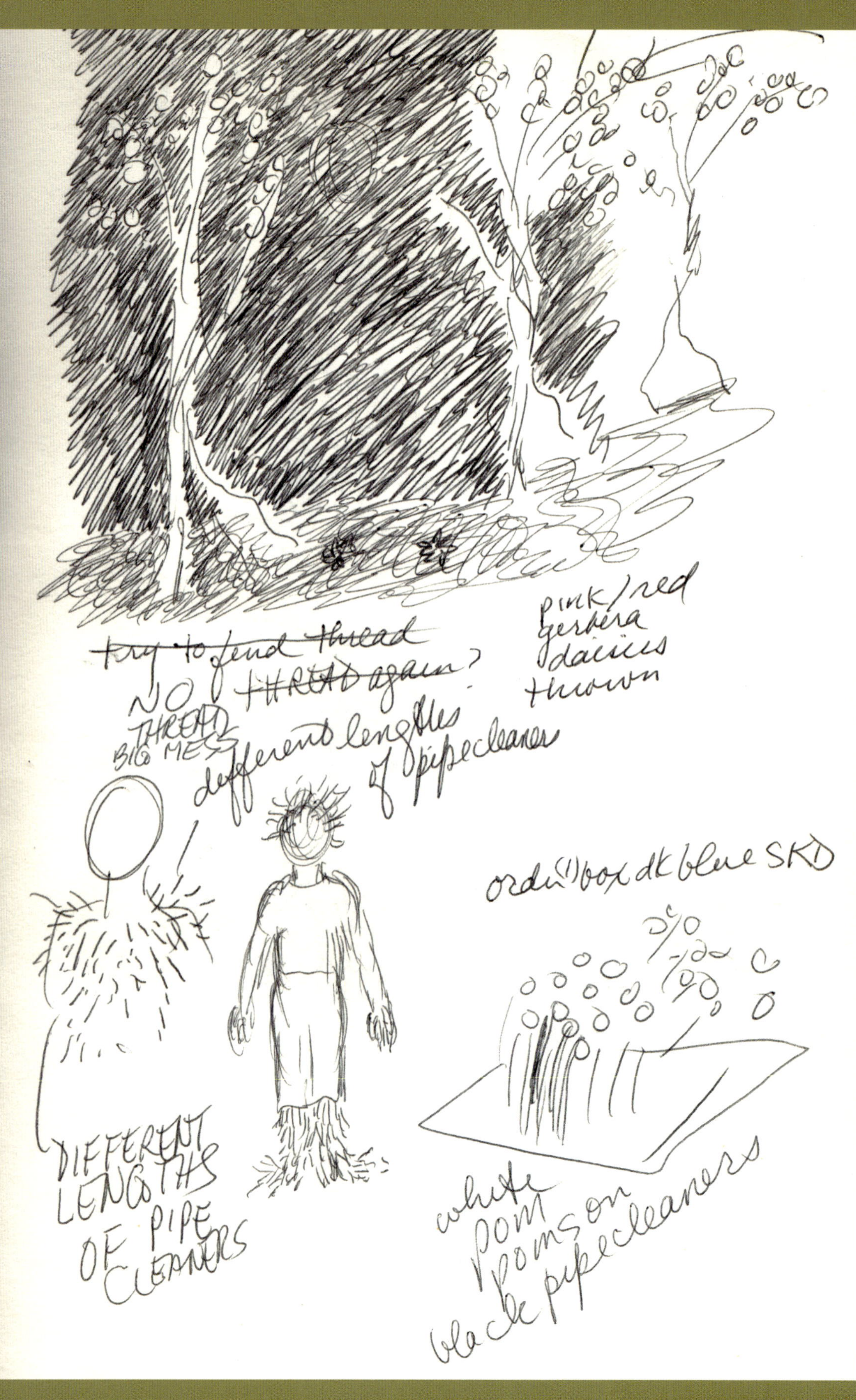
try to fend thread
NO THREAD again?
THREAD
BIG MESS
different lengths of pipecleaner
pink/red gerbera daisies thrown
ordin'l box dk blue SKD
DIFFERENT LENGTHS OF PIPE CLEANERS
white pom poms on black pipecleaners

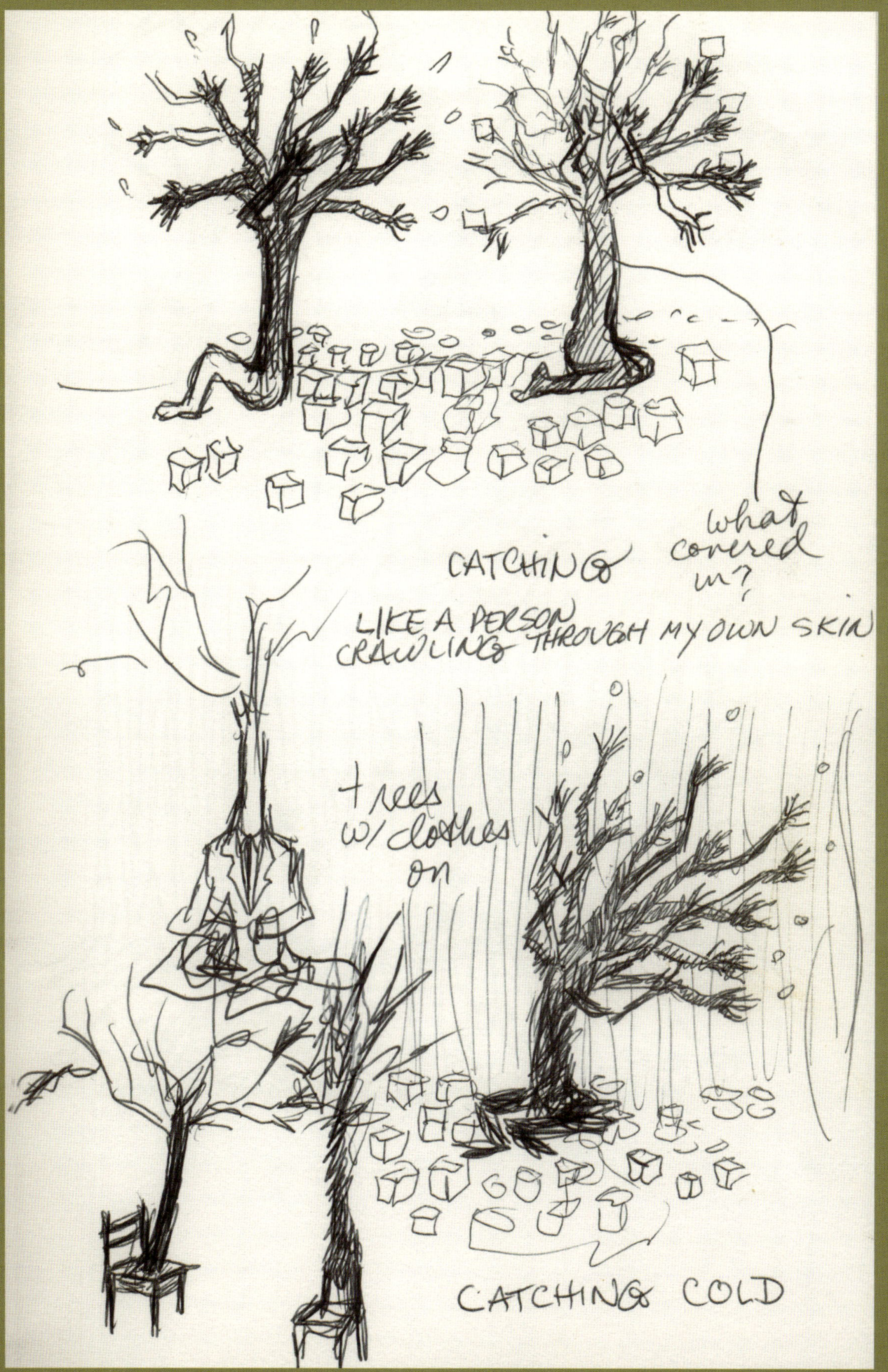

CATCHING
what covered in?
LIKE A PERSON CRAWLING THROUGH MY OWN SKIN
trees w/ clothes on
CATCHING COLD

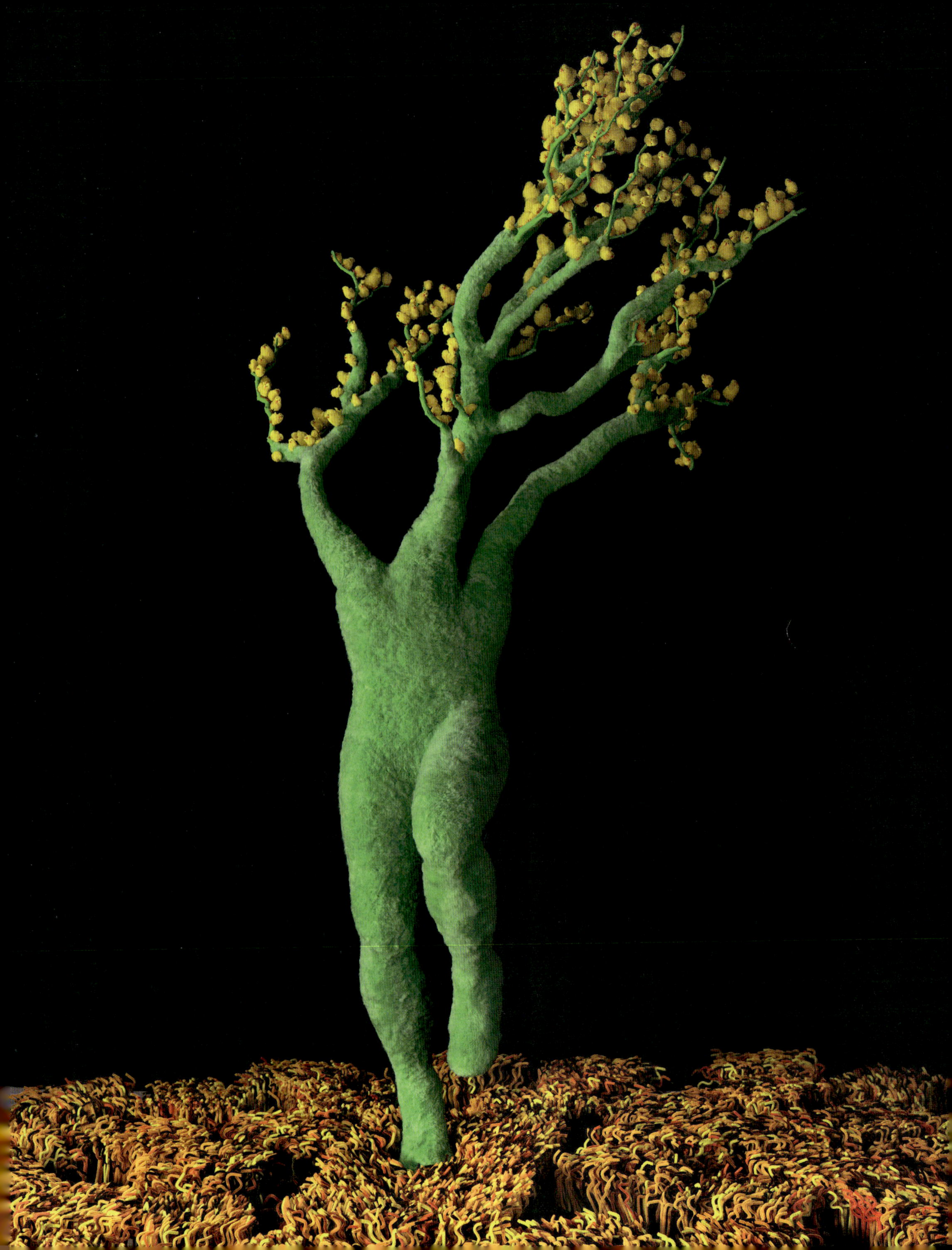

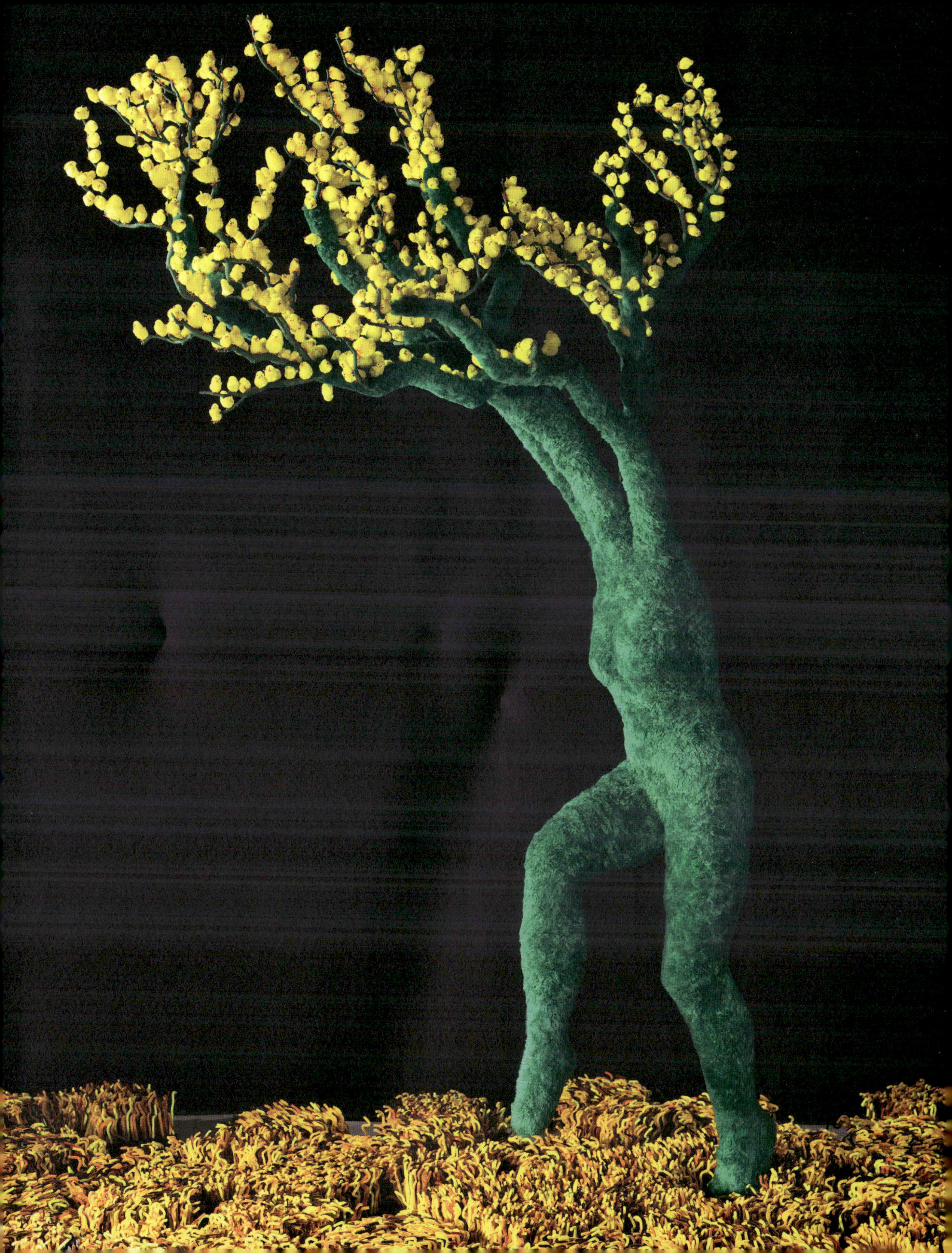

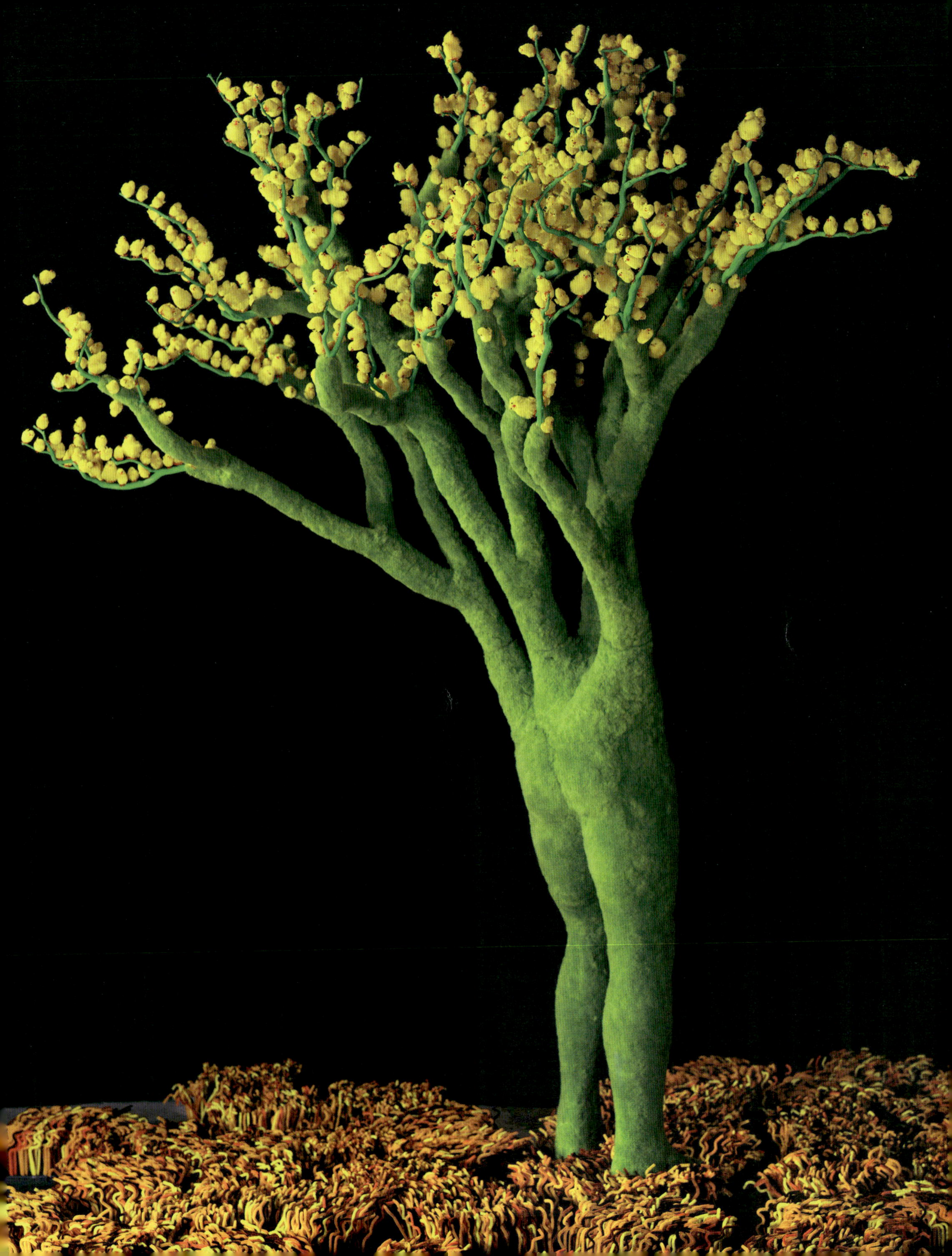

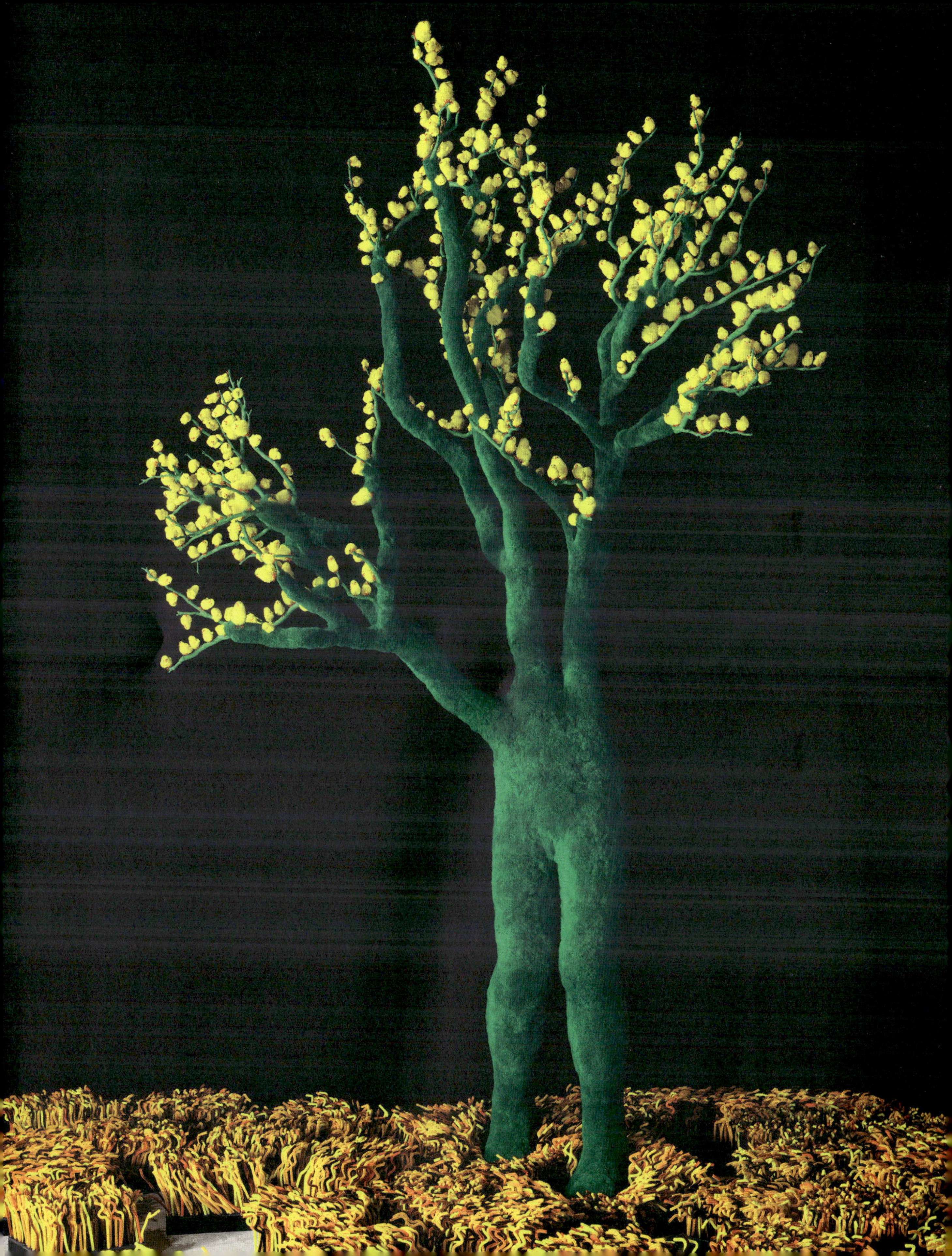

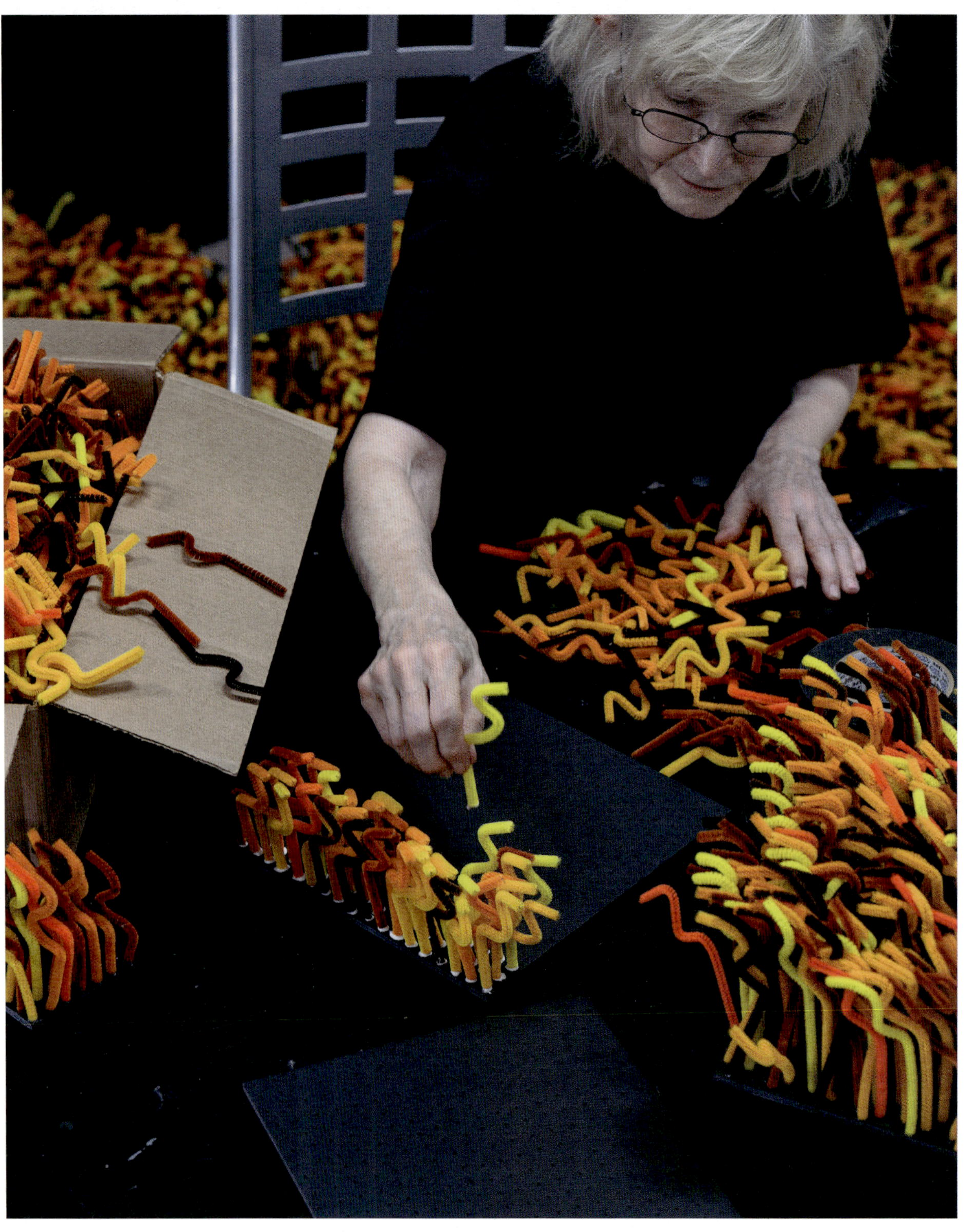

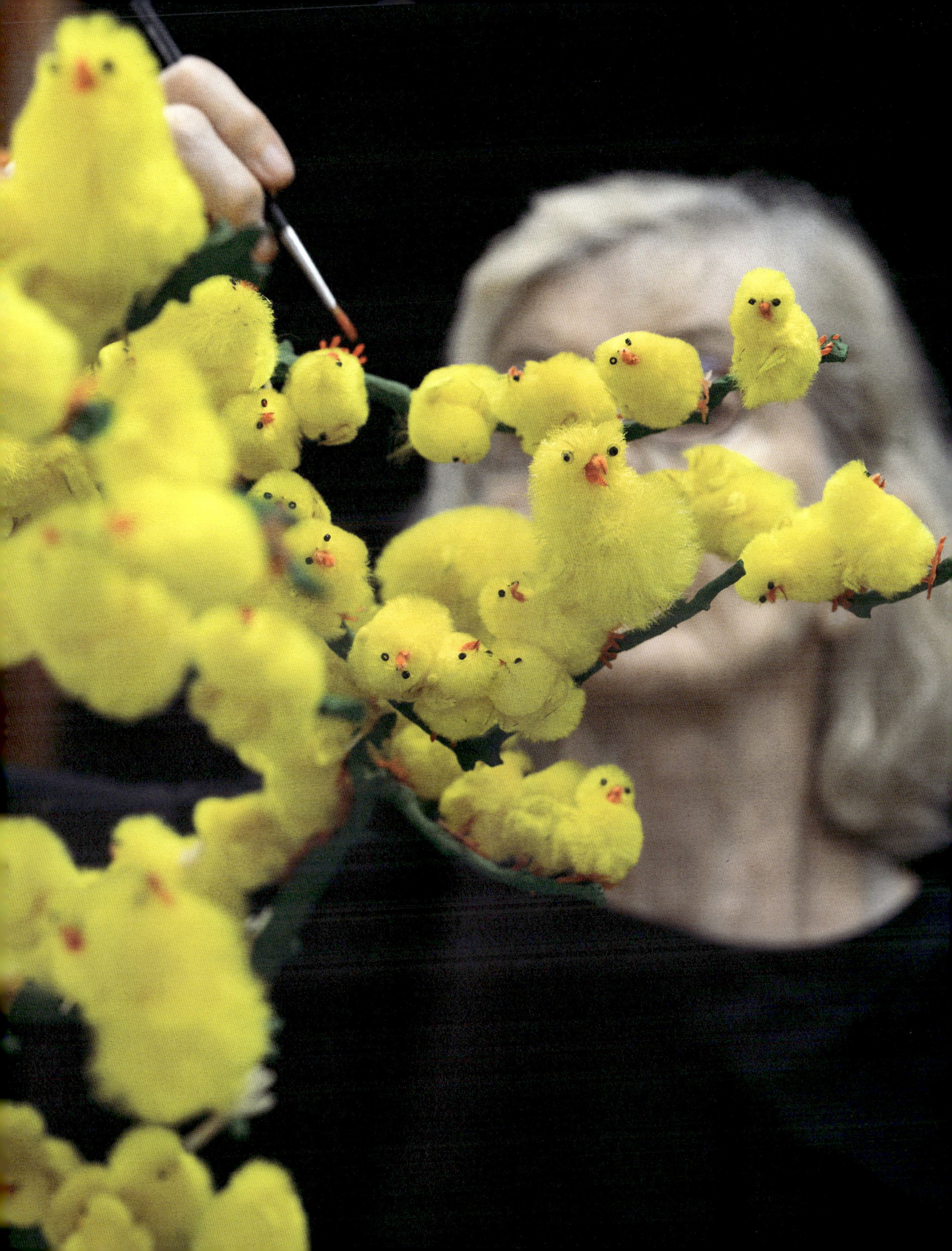

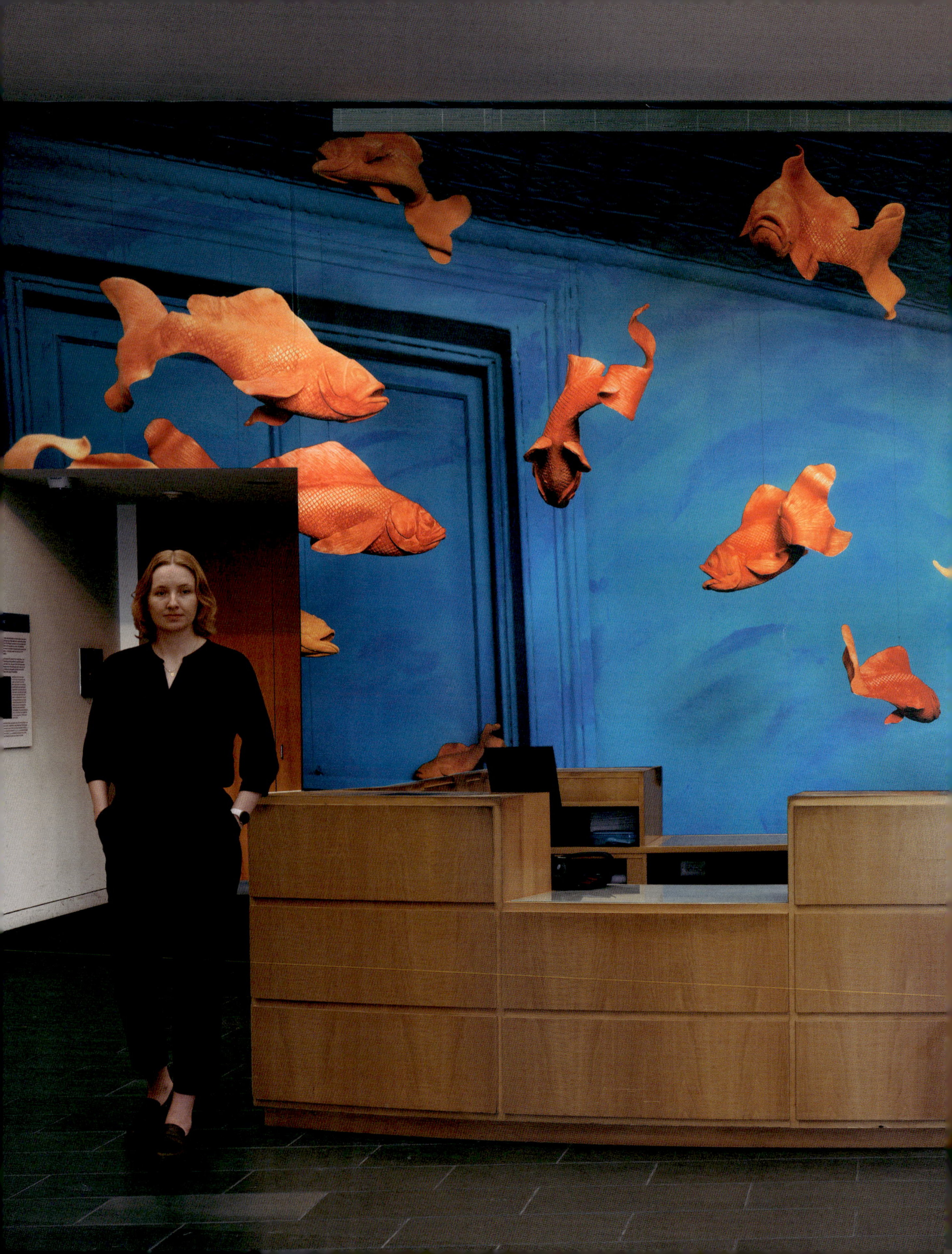

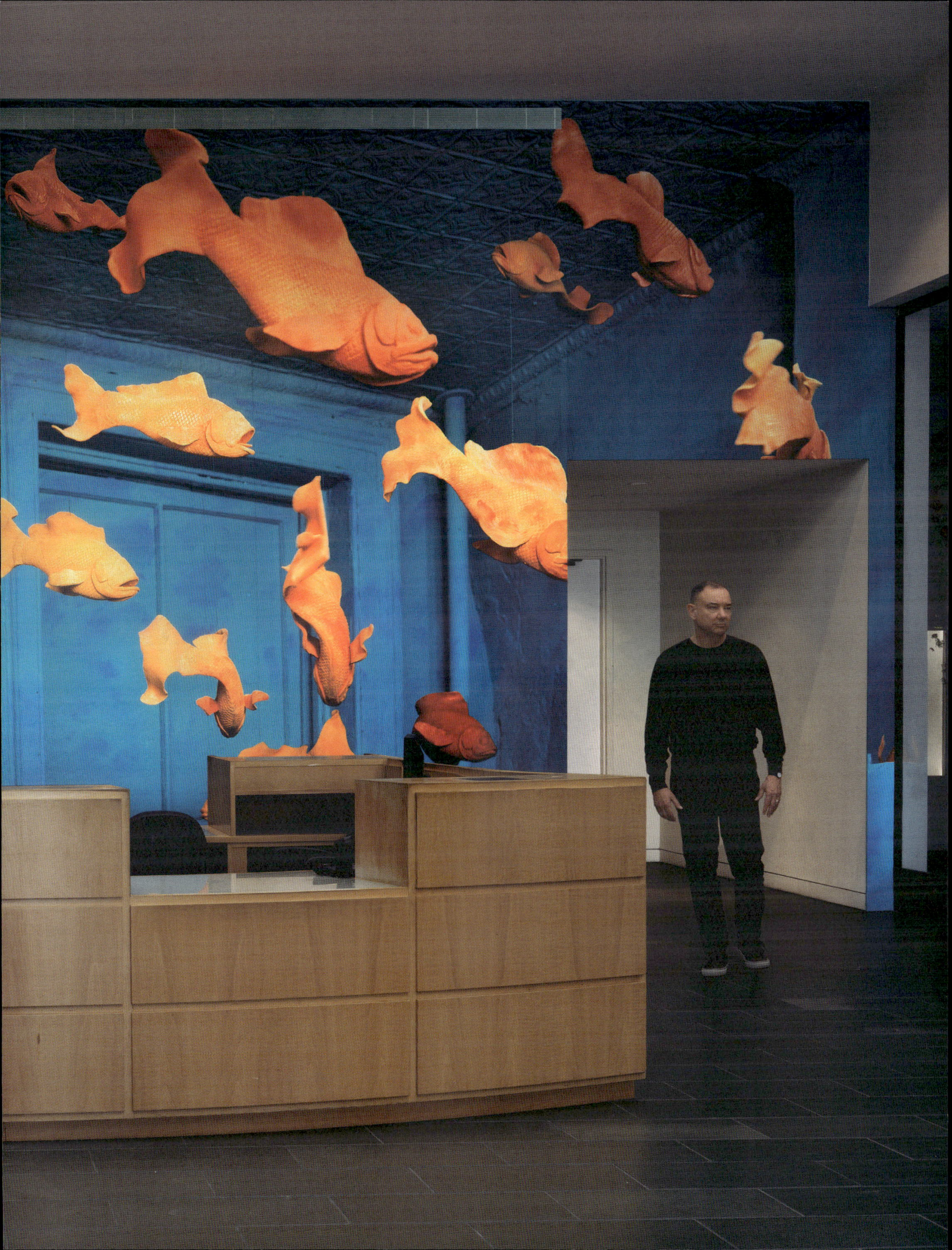

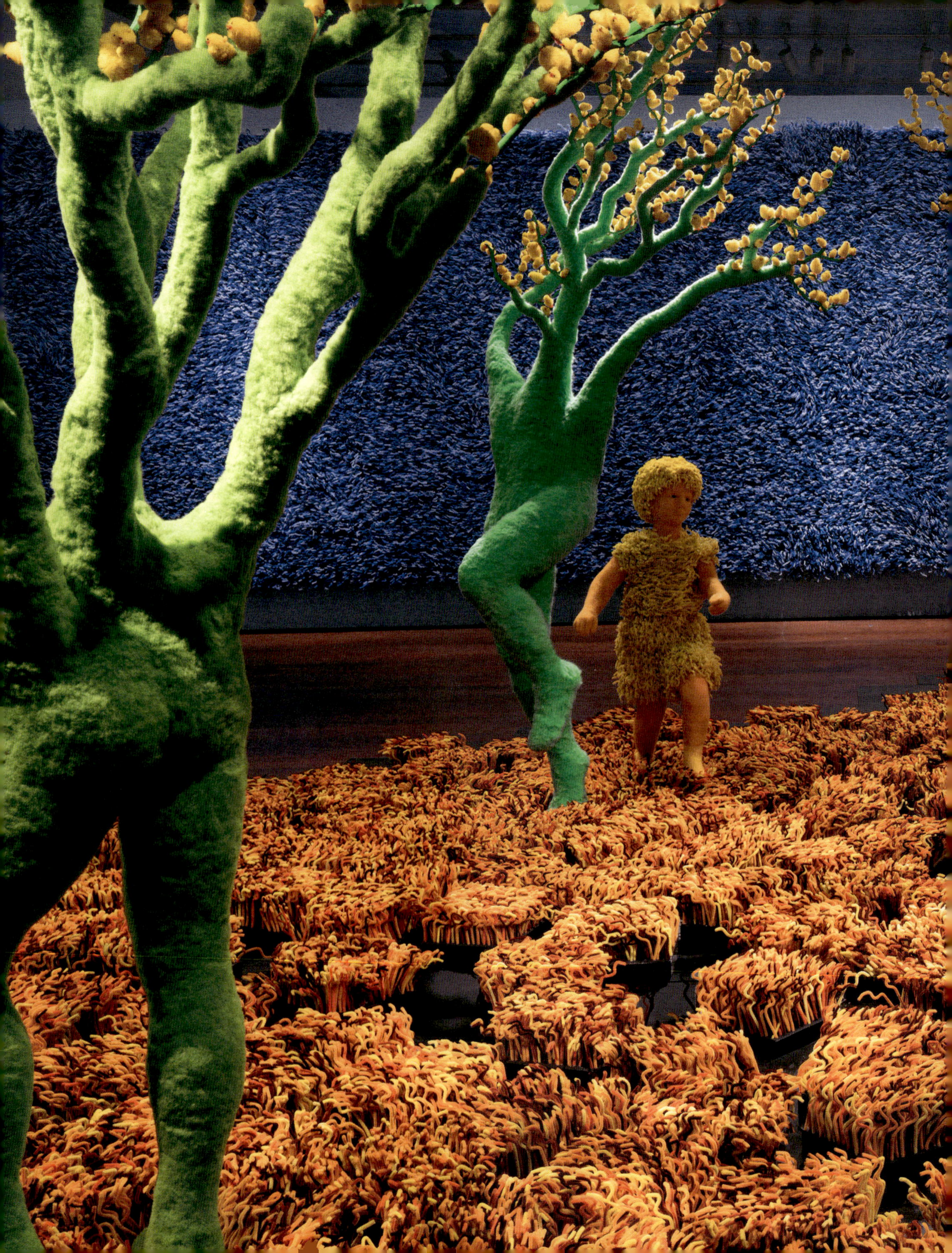

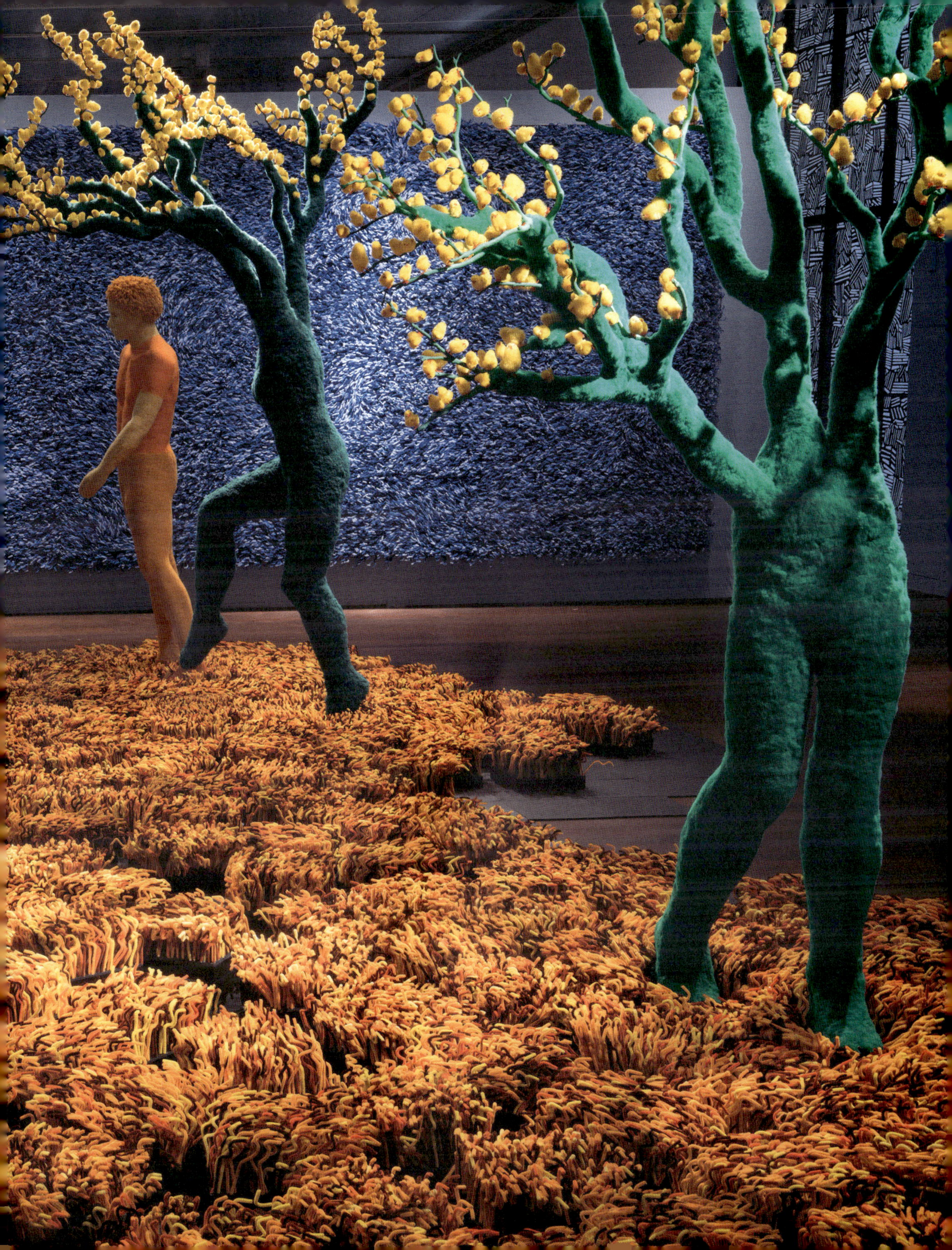

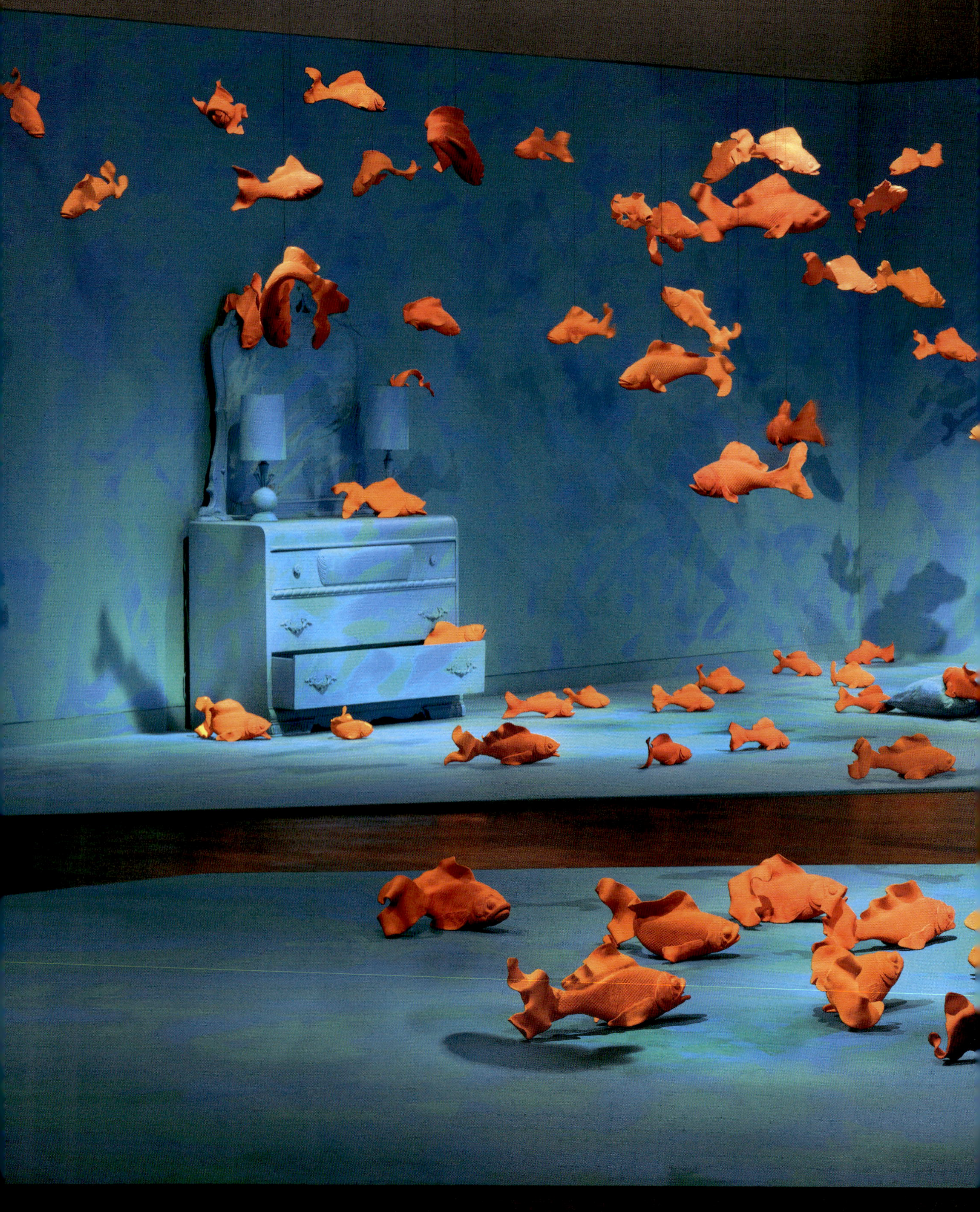

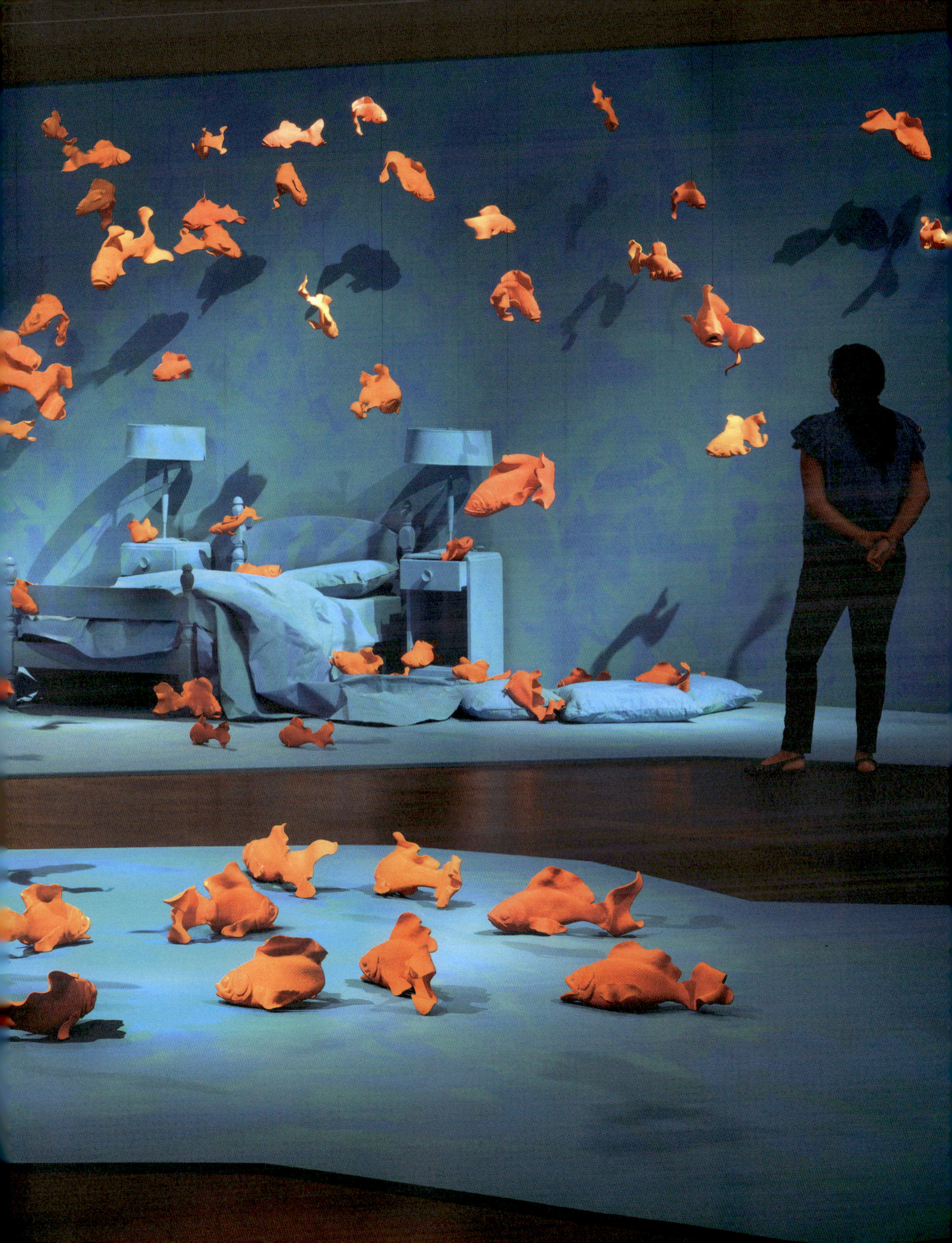

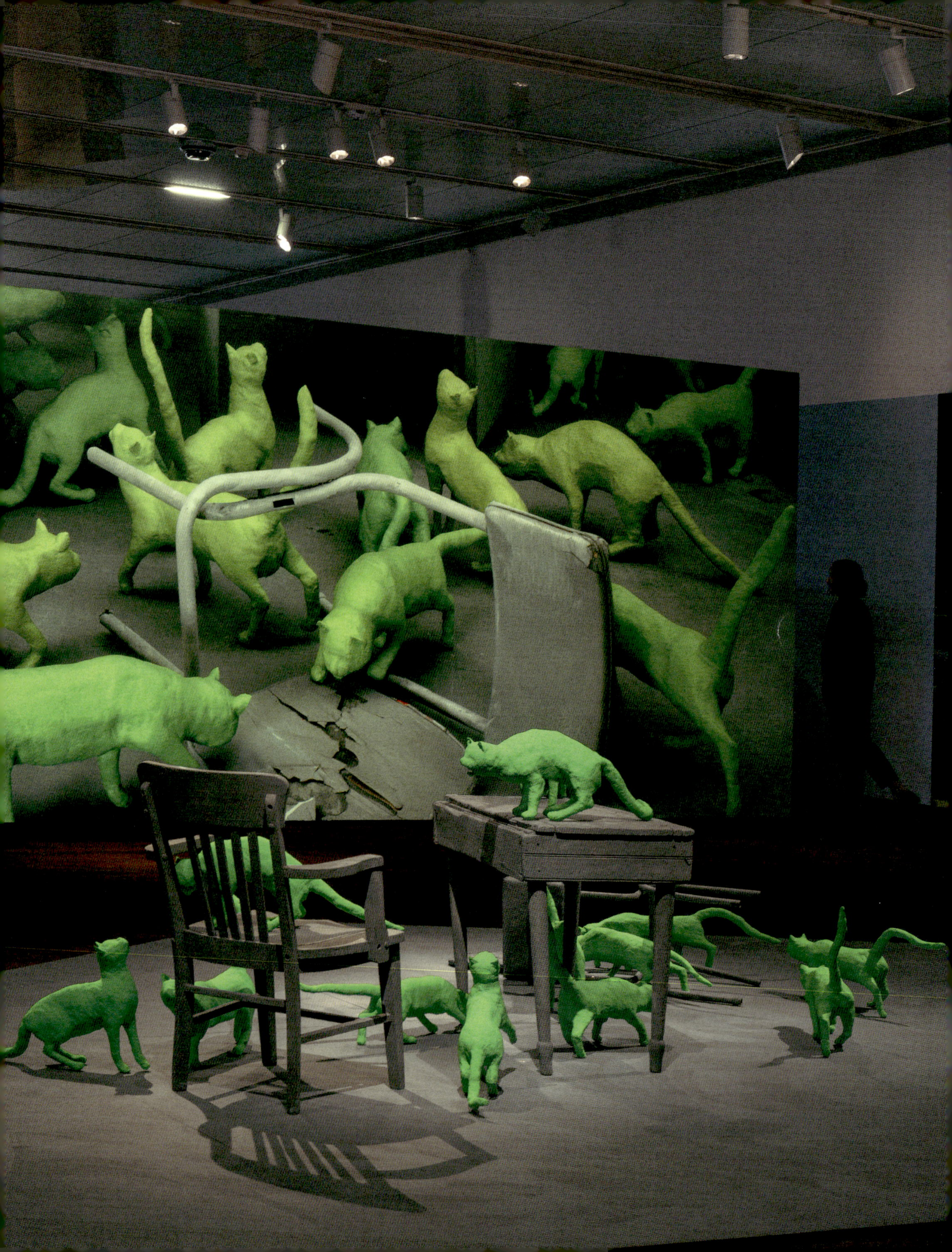

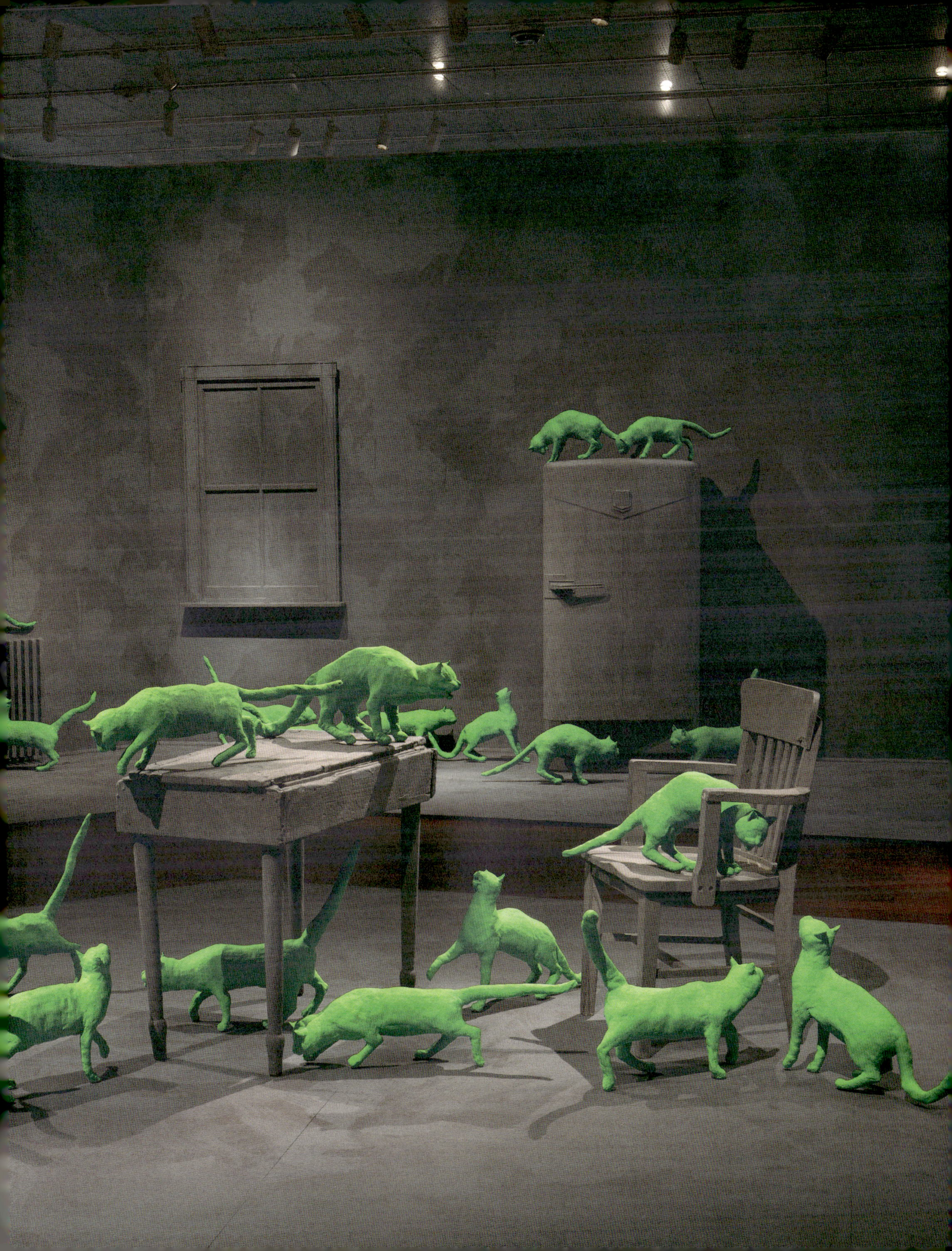

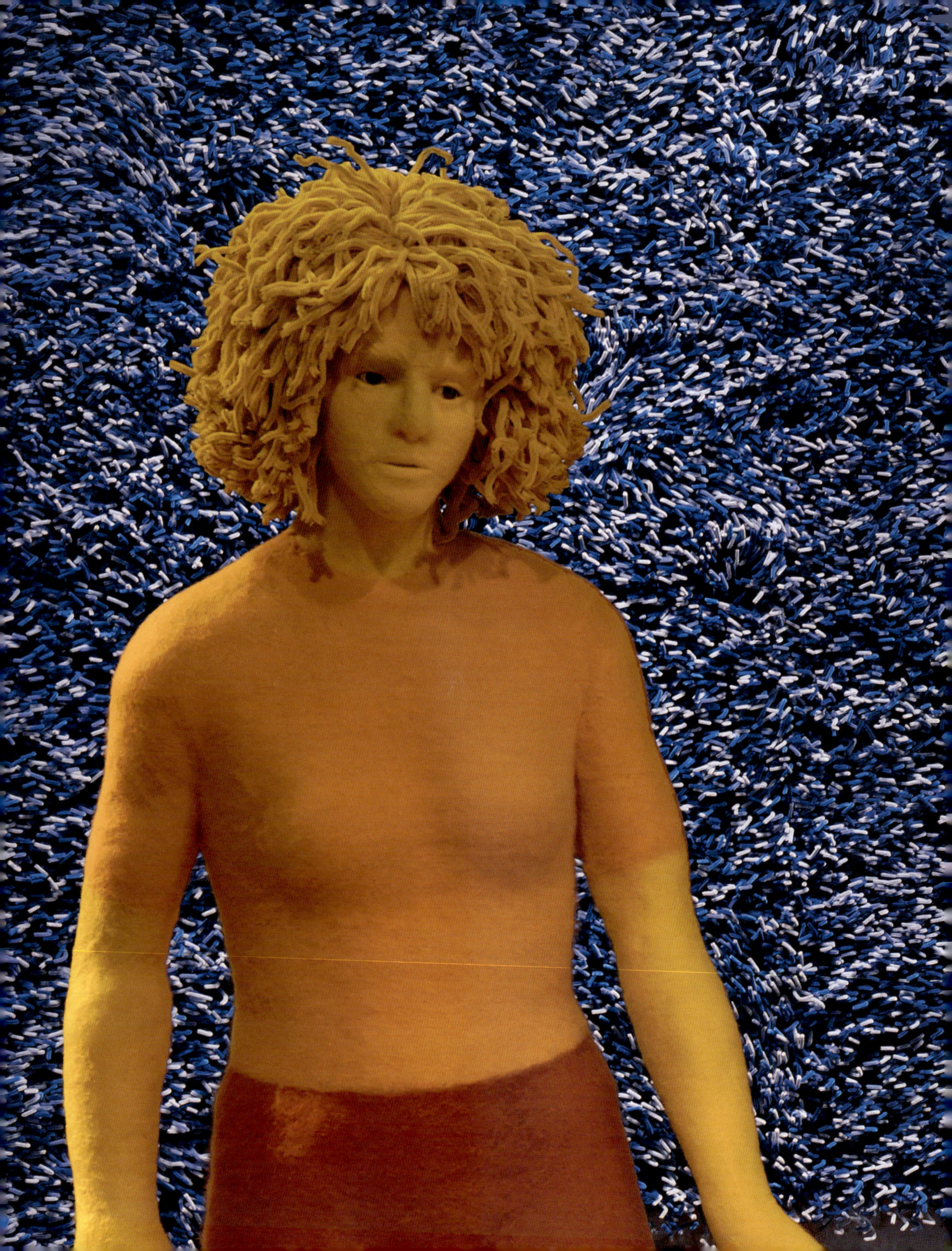

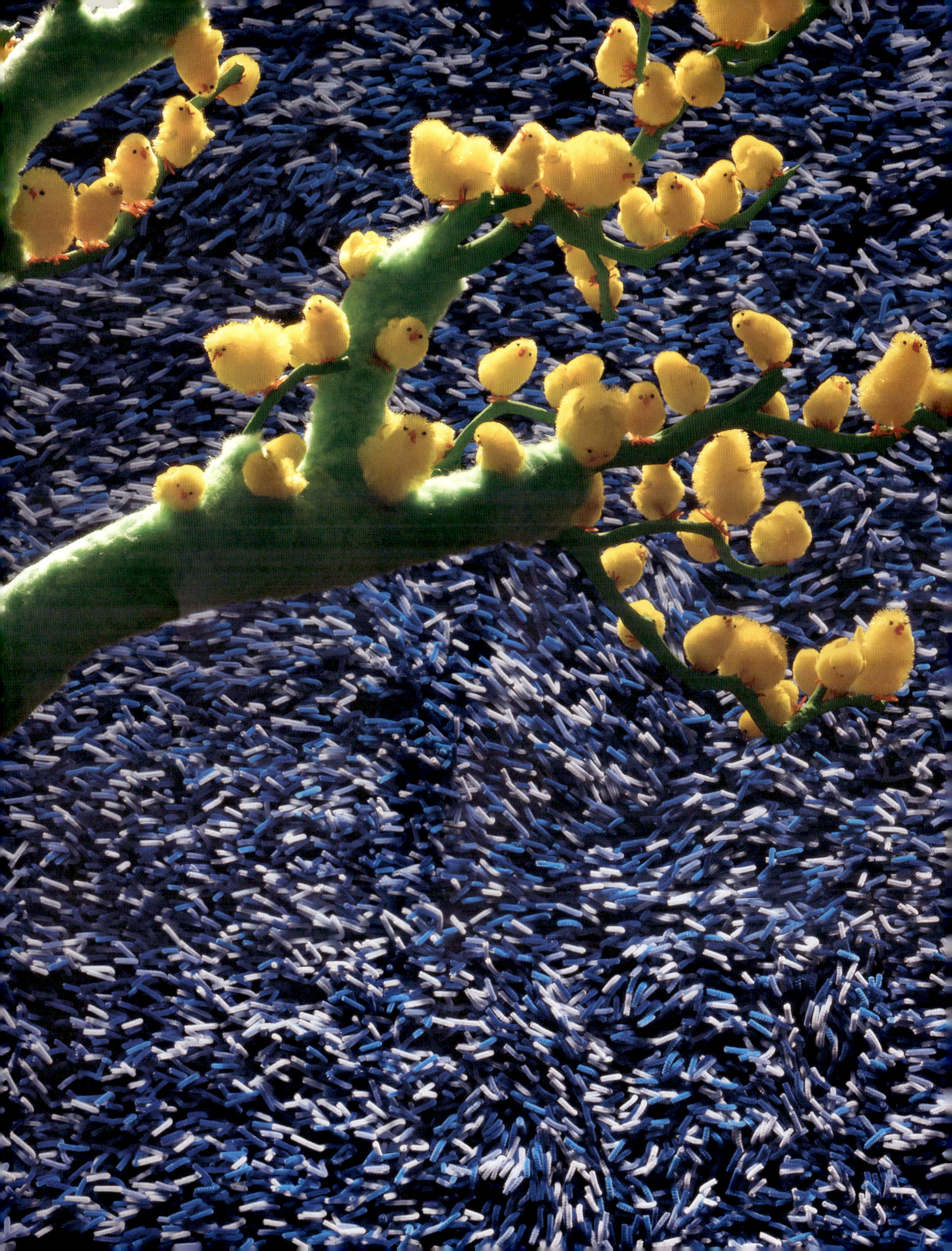

Artist Biography

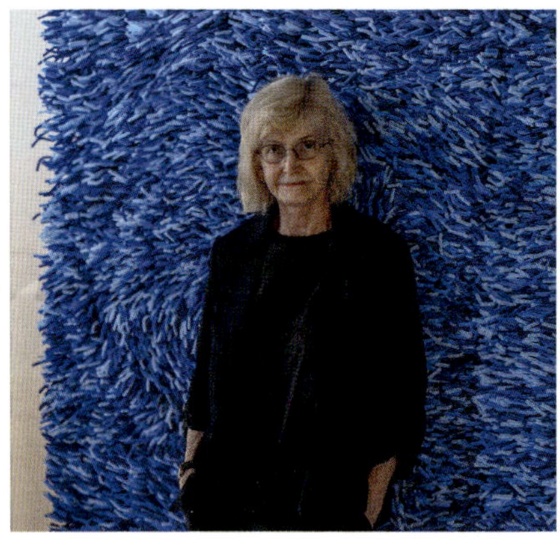

Sandy Skoglund was born in 1946 in Weymouth, Massachusetts, to a Scottish mother and a Swedish father. At the age of 3, Skoglund and her younger brother were hospitalized and quarantined with polio on a ship anchored in Boston Bay. Skoglund was treated during early childhood due to paralysis of her left shoulder.

Skoglund's family moved frequently due to her father's corporate job transfers. The early years were spent in Massachusetts, Maine, and Connecticut, followed by California and Michigan. During summers, she worked various jobs, including the Space Bar in Disneyland's Tomorrowland and later decorating cakes on a Detroit bakery assembly line.

From 1964 to 1968, Skoglund studied studio art and art history at Smith College, participating in a study abroad program in France. Studying art history at the Sorbonne ignited her interest in avant-garde cinema, especially *Cahiers du Cinema* and the French New Wave's auteur theory.

After graduating with a BA in 1968, Skoglund earned money for graduate school teaching junior high art in Illinois. The following year, she went to the University of Iowa to study painting, art conservation, printmaking, filmmaking, and multimedia. She graduated in 1972 with an MA and an MFA degree in painting.

A month after graduation, Skoglund moved to New York City. Her evolving interest in multimedia led to a focus on conceptual art. Skoglund's work at that time involved repetitive and accumulative gestures derived from a minimalist philosophy resulting in works that "made themselves" over time.

Duplication as a visual strategy is seen in her photocopying on a rented Xerox machine in her apartment in 1974, and later her 1975 *Performance with Jellybeans*. Important figures in 1970s avant-garde cinema like Michael Snow and his use of serialism inspired Skoglund to use photography to document the many nearly identical New England motel cabins along the coastline. These deadpan images forecast themes of similarity and difference that run throughout her work.

Skoglund's desire to accurately document conceptual ideas led her to a deeper appreciation of the camera and still photography. Learning more about film techniques prompted her interest in advertising images and popular culture, which yielded Skoglund's 1978 still life series of food. These images had titles like *Peas on a Plate* and *Luncheon Meat on a Counter*, which she described as "commercially uncommercial."

Wanting to put her hand in front of the camera, in 1980 Skoglund combined her handmade sculptures, live models, and photography for the image *Radioactive Cats*. With this piece, Skoglund launched her multimedia practice of creating elaborate installations and photographs that immerse the viewer in an alternate reality.

One year later, Skoglund reprised the themes of serialism, repetition, and similarity with *Revenge of the Goldfish*, a room-sized installation and photograph that includes 119 individually handcrafted ceramic goldfish made over a period of six months. *Radioactive Cats* and *Revenge of the Goldfish* are two defining images of the staged photography movement of the 1980s and 90s.

Since the 80s, Skoglund has developed her vision as a conceptual photographer and installation artist with extraordinary tableaux that provide viewers with unexpected visual sensations. Her striking use of elaborate sets, hand-sculpted creatures, and live models has spawned unique images rich in conceptual and physical complexity. With unusual materials, striking color palettes, and clashes between nature and artifice, Skoglund invites the viewer into a compelling world of psychological suspense, provoking questions and leaving lasting impressions.

Skoglund lived in New York City until 2003, when she relocated to Jersey City, New Jersey.

List of Images

Front cover, page 32: *Early Morning* from *The Outtakes* series 1981/2021 (details)

Opposite title page, pages 2, 4—5, 7—13, 46—51, back cover: *Fresh Hybrid* studio views, 2025

Page 14: *The Company of Others* from *The Outtakes* series, 1990/2021 (detail)

Page 15: *Beyond the Door* from *The Outtakes* series, 1980/2021

Page 16: *Angels and Strangers* from *The Outtakes* series, 1991/2021 (detail)

Page 17: *Chasing Chaos* from *The Outtakes* series, 1987/2021

Page 18: *Wishes and Whispers* from *The Outtakes* series, 1994/2021

Page 19: *The Wild Inside* from *The Outtakes* series, 1980/2021 (detail)

Page 20: *Beyond the Door* from *The Outtakes* series, 1980/2021 (detail)

Page 21: *The Company of Others* from *The Outtakes* series, 1990/2021

Page 22: *Angels and Strangers* from *The Outtakes* series, 1991/2021

Page 23: *Chasing Chaos* from *The Outtakes* series 1987/2021 (detail)

Page 24: *The Conversation* from *The Outtakes* series, 1992/2021 (detail)

Page 25: *Early Morning* from *The Outtakes* series, 1981/2021

Page 26: *The Wild Inside* from *The Outtakes* series, 1980/2021

Page 27: *Wishes and Whispers* from *The Outtakes* series, 1994/2021 (detail)

Page 28: *Natural Havoc* from *The Outtakes* series, 2008/2025 (detail)

Page 29: *Catching Chance* from *The Outtakes* series, 2000/2021

Page 30: *The Paper Sink* from *The Outtakes* series, 1997/2021

Page 31: *Sticky Thrills* from *The Outtakes* series, 1998/2021 (detail)

Page 33: *The Conversation* from *The Outtakes* series, 1992/2021

Page 34: *Catching Chance* from *The Outtakes* series, 2000/2021 (detail)

Page 35: *Natural Havoc* from *The Outtakes* series 2008/2025

Page 36: *Sticky Thrills* from *The Outtakes* series, 1998/2021

Page 37: *Warm Frost* from *The Outtakes* series, 2001/2021 (detail)

Page 38: *The Paper Sink* from *The Outtakes* series, 1997/2021

Page 39: *Warm Frost* from *The Outtakes* series, 2001/2021

Pages 40—45: Notebook sketches, 1979—2008

Pages 52—61: *Sandy Skoglund: Enchanting Nature*, McNay Art Museum, San Antonio, Texas, September 11, 2025—February 1, 2026

Page 62: Sandy Skoglund self-portrait, 2025

Sandy Skoglund
Enchanting Nature

© Artworks, Sandy Skoglund
© Introduction, René Paul Barilleaux
© Conversation, Laura van Straaten

This book is published by Damiani Books in collaboration with McNay Art Museum and Paci Contemporary on the occasion of the exhibition, *Sandy Skoglund: Enchanting Nature*, organized by McNay Art Museum in San Antonio, Texas, USA, from September 11, 2025 to February 1, 2026.

Published by Damiani Books
info@damianibooks.com
www.damianibooks.com

All rights reserved. No part of this publication may be reproduced or transmitted in any form or by any means, electronic or mechanical—including photocopying, recording or by any information storage or retrieval system—without prior permission in writing from the publisher.

Printed in September 2025, Italy.

ISBN 978-88-6208-851-0

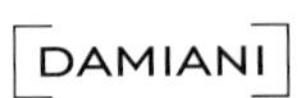
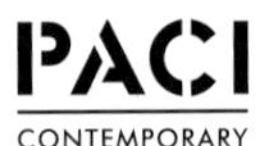
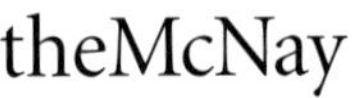